Cesar Chavez

Consulting Editors

Rodolfo Cardona
professor of Spanish
and comparative literature,
Boston University

James Cockcroft
visiting professor of Latin American
and Caribbean studies,
State University of New York at Albany

Hispanics of Achievement

Cesar Chavez

Consuelo Rodriguez

Chelsea House Publishers
Philadelphia

CHELSEA HOUSE PUBLISHERS

Editor-in-Chief: Remmel Nunn
Managing Editor: Karyn Gullen Browne
Copy Chief: Juliann Barbato
Picture Editor: Adrian G. Allen
Art Director: Maria Epes
Deputy Copy Chief: Mark Rifkin
Assistant Art Director: Noreen Romano
Manufacturing Manager: Gerald Levine
Systems Manager: Lindsey Ottman
Production Manager: Joseph Romano
Production Coordinator: Marie Claire Cebrián

Hispanics of Achievement
Senior Editor: John W. Selfridge

Staff for CESAR CHAVEZ
Associate Editor: Philip Koslow
Copy Editor: Joseph Roman
Editorial Assistant: Martin Mooney
Picture Researcher: Wendy P. Wills
Cover Illustration: Steven Parton

9

Library of Congress Cataloging-in-Publication Data
Rodriguez, Consuelo
   Cesar Chavez/Consuelo Rodriguez
      p. cm.—(Hispanics of achievement)
   Includes bibliographical references and index.
   Summary: Biography of the Mexican-American labor activist who
organized and led the migrant farm workers in their struggle for bet-
ter working conditions.
   ISBN 0-7910-1232-8
         0-7910-1259-X (pbk.)
   1. Chavez, Cesar, 1927– —Juvenile literature. 2. United Farm
Workers—History—Juvenile literature. 3. Trade-unions—Migrant
agricultural laborers—United States—Officials and employees—
Biography—Juvenile literature. 4. Mexican Americans—Biography—Juvenile literature. [1. Chavez, Cesar, 1927– . 2. Labor
unions—Biography. 3. Mexican Americans—Biography 4. United
Farm Workers—History. 5. Migrant labor.] I. Title II. Series
HD6509.C48G37 1991
331.88'13'092—dc20   90-42171
[B]   CIP
[92]   AC

Contents

HISPANICS OF ACHIEVEMENT

JOAN BAEZ
Mexican-American folksinger

RUBÉN BLADES
Panamanian lawyer and entertainer

JORGE LUIS BORGES
Argentine writer

PABLO CASALS
Spanish cellist and conductor

MIGUEL DE CERVANTES
Spanish writer

CESAR CHAVEZ
Mexican-American labor leader

JULIO CÉSAR CHÁVEZ
Mexican boxing champion

EL CID
Spanish military leader

HENRY CISNEROS
Mexican-American political leader

ROBERTO CLEMENTE
Puerto Rican baseball player

SALVADOR DALÍ
Spanish painter

PLÁCIDO DOMINGO
Spanish singer

GLORIA ESTEFAN
Cuban-American singer

GABRIEL GARCÍA MÁRQUEZ
Colombian writer

FRANCISCO JOSÉ DE GOYA
Spanish painter

JULIO IGLESIAS
Spanish singer

RAUL JULIA
Puerto Rican actor

FRIDA KAHLO
Mexican painter

JOSÉ MARTÍ
Cuban revolutionary and poet

RITA MORENO
Puerto Rican singer and actress

PABLO NERUDA
Chilean poet and diplomat

OCTAVIO PAZ
Mexican poet and critic

PABLO PICASSO
Spanish artist

ANTHONY QUINN
Mexican-American actor

DIEGO RIVERA
Mexican painter

LINDA RONSTADT
Mexican-American singer

ANTONIO LÓPEZ DE SANTA ANNA
Mexican general and politician

GEORGE SANTAYANA
Spanish philosopher and poet

JUNÍPERO SERRA
Spanish missionary and explorer

LEE TREVINO
Mexican-American golfer

PANCHO VILLA
Mexican revolutionary

CHELSEA HOUSE PUBLISHERS

INTRODUCTION

Hispanics of Achievement

Rodolfo Cardona

The Spanish language and many other elements of Spanish culture are present in the United States today and have been since the country's earliest beginnings. Some of these elements have come directly from the Iberian Peninsula; others have come indirectly, by way of Mexico, the Caribbean basin, and the countries of Central and South America.

Spanish culture has influenced America in many subtle ways, and consequently many Americans remain relatively unaware of the extent of its impact. The vast majority of them recognize the influence of Spanish culture in America, but they often do not realize the great importance and long history of that influence. This is partly because Americans have tended to judge the Hispanic influence in the United States in statistical terms rather than to look closely at the ways in which individual Hispanics have profoundly affected American culture. For this reason, it is fitting that Americans obtain more than a passing acquaintance with the origins of these Spanish cultural elements and gain an understanding of how they have been woven into the fabric of American society.

It is well documented that Spanish seafarers were the first to explore and colonize many of the early territories of what is today called the United States of America. For this reason, students of geography discover Hispanic names all over the map of the United States. For instance, the Strait of Juan de Fuca was named after the Spanish explorer who first navigated the waters of the Pacific Northwest; the names of states such as Arizona (arid zone), Montana (mountain), Florida (thus named because it was reached on Easter Sunday, which in Spanish is called the feast of Pascua Florida), and California (named after a fictitious land in one of the first and probably the most popular among the Spanish novels of chivalry, *Amadis of Gaul*) are all derived from Spanish; and there are numerous mountains, rivers, canyons, towns, and cities with Spanish names throughout the United States.

Not only explorers but many other illustrious figures in Spanish history have helped define American culture. For example, the 13th-century king of Spain Alfonso X, also known as the Learned, may be unknown to the majority of Americans, but his work on the codification of Spanish law has greatly influenced the evolution of American law, particularly in the jurisdictions of the Southwest. For this contribution a statue of him stands in the rotunda of the Capitol in Washington, D.C. Likewise, the name Diego Rivera may be unfamiliar to most Americans, but this Mexican painter influenced many American artists whose paintings, commissioned during the Great Depression and the New Deal era of the 1930s, adorn the walls of government buildings throughout the United States. In recent years the contributions of Puerto Ricans, Mexicans, Mexican Americans (Chicanos), and Cubans in American cities such as Boston, Chicago, Los Angeles,

Miami, Minneapolis, New York, and San Antonio have been enormous.

The importance of the Spanish language in this vast cultural complex cannot be overstated. Spanish, after all, is second only to English as the most widely spoken of Western languages within the United States as well as in the entire world. The popularity of the Spanish language in America has a long history.

In addition to Spanish exploration of the New World, the great Spanish literary tradition served as a vehicle for bringing the language and culture to America. Interest in Spanish literature in America began when English immigrants brought with them translations of Spanish masterpieces of the Golden Age. As early as 1683, private libraries in Philadelphia and Boston contained copies of the first picaresque novel, *Lazarillo de Tormes*, translations of Francisco de Quevedo's *Los Sueños*, and copies of the immortal epic of reality and illusion *Don Quixote*, by the great Spanish writer Miguel de Cervantes. It would not be surprising if Cotton Mather, the arch-Puritan, read *Don Quixote* in its original Spanish, if only to enrich his vocabulary in preparation for his writing *La fe del cristiano en 24 artículos de la Institución de Cristo, enviada a los españoles para que abran sus ojos* (The Christian's Faith in 24 Articles of the Institution of Christ, Sent to the Spaniards to Open Their Eyes), published in Boston in 1699.

Over the years, Spanish authors and their works have had a vast influence on American literature—from Washington Irving, John Steinbeck, and Ernest Hemingway in the novel to Henry Wadsworth Longfellow and Archibald MacLeish in poetry. Such important American writers as James Fenimore Cooper, Edgar Allan Poe, Walt Whitman, Mark Twain, and Herman Melville all owe a sizable debt to the Spanish literary tradition. Some writers, such as Willa Cather and Maxwell Anderson, who explored Spanish themes they came into contact with in the American Southwest and Mexico, were influenced less directly but no less profoundly.

Important contributions to a knowledge of Spanish culture in the United States were also made by many lesser known individuals—teachers, publishers, historians, entrepreneurs, and others—with a love for Spanish culture. One of the most significant of these contributions was made by Abiel Smith, a Harvard College graduate of the class of 1764, when he bequeathed stock worth $20,000 to Harvard for the support of a professor of French and Spanish. By 1819 this endowment had produced enough income to appoint a professor, and the philologist and humanist George Ticknor became the first holder of the Abiel Smith Chair, which was the very first endowed Chair at Harvard University. Other illustrious holders of the Smith Chair would include the poets Henry Wadsworth Longfellow and James Russell Lowell.

A highly respected teacher and scholar, Ticknor was also a collector of Spanish books, and as such he made a very special contribution to America's knowledge of Spanish culture. He was instrumental in amassing for Harvard libraries one of the first and most impressive collections of Spanish books in the United States. He also had a valuable personal collection of Spanish books and manuscripts, which he bequeathed to the Boston Public Library.

With the creation of the Abiel Smith Chair, Spanish language and literature courses became part of the curriculum at Harvard, which also went on to become the first American university to offer graduate studies in Romance languages. Other colleges and universities throughout the United States gradually followed Harvard's example, and today Spanish language and culture may be studied at most American institutions of higher learning.

No discussion of the Spanish influence in the United States, however brief, would be complete without a mention of the Spanish influence on art. Important American artists such as John Singer Sargent, James A. M. Whistler, Thomas Eakins, and Mary Cassatt all explored Spanish subjects and experimented with Spanish techniques. Virtually every serious American artist living today has studied the work of the Spanish masters as well as the great 20th-century Spanish painters Salvador Dalí, Joan Miró, and Pablo Picasso.

The most pervasive Spanish influence in America, however, has probably been in music. Compositions such as Leonard Bernstein's *West Side Story*, the Latinization of William Shakespeare's *Romeo and Juliet* set in New York's Puerto Rican quarter, and Aaron Copland's *Salon Mexico* are two obvious examples. In general, one can hear the influence of Latin rhythms—from tango to mambo, from guaracha to salsa—in virtually every form of American music.

This series of biographies, which Chelsea House has published under the general title HISPANICS OF ACHIEVEMENT, constitutes further recognition of—and a renewed effort to bring forth to the consciousness of America's young people—the contributions that Hispanic people have made not only in the United States but throughout the civilized world. The men and women who are featured in this series have attained a high level of accomplishment in their respective fields of endeavor and have made a permanent mark on American society.

The title of this series must be understood in its broadest possible sense: The term *Hispanics* is intended to include Spaniards, Spanish Americans, and individuals from many countries whose language and culture have either direct or indirect Spanish origins. The names of many of the people included in this series will be immediately familiar; others will be less recognizable. All, however, have attained recognition within their own countries, and often their fame has transcended their borders.

The series HISPANICS OF ACHIEVEMENT thus addresses the attainments and struggles of Hispanic people in the United States and seeks to tell the stories of individuals whose personal and professional lives in some way reflect the larger Hispanic experience. These stories are exemplary of what human beings can accomplish, often against daunting odds and by extraordinary personal sacrifice, where there is conviction and determination.

Fray Junípero Serra, the 18th-century Spanish Franciscan missionary, is one such individual. Although in very poor health, he
devoted the last 15 years of his life to the foundation of missions
throughout California—then a mostly unsettled expanse of land—
in an effort to bring a better life to Native Americans through the
cultivation of crafts and animal husbandry. An example from
recent times, the Mexican-American labor leader Cesar Chavez
has battled bitter opposition and made untold personal sacrifices
in his effort to help poor agricultural workers who have been
exploited for decades on farms throughout the Southwest.

The talent with which each one of these men and women may
have been endowed required dedication and hard work to develop
and become fully realized. Many of them have enjoyed rewards
for their efforts during their own lifetime, whereas others have
died poor and unrecognized. For some it took a long time to
achieve their goals, for others success came at an early age, and for
still others the struggle continues. All of them, however, stand out
as people whose lives have made a difference, whose achieve-
ments we need to recognize today and should continue to honor
in the future.

Cesar Chavez

Senator Robert F. Kennedy breaks bread with Cesar Chavez on March 10, 1968, during the mass marking the end of Chavez's 25-day fast. Chavez went without food to emphasize the spiritual and nonviolent nature of the farm workers' strike against California's grape growers.

CHAPTER ONE

"So I Stopped Eating"

On March 10, 1968, 4,000 people filled a county park in Delano, California. Most of them were farm workers: Mexican Americans, Mexicans, Puerto Ricans, Filipinos, blacks, southern whites. Since 1965, they had been on strike against California's grape growers. But they had not come to the park to attend a meeting of their union, the United Farm Workers Organizing Committee (UFWOC). They had come to attend a mass. A makeshift altar had been set up on a flatbed truck in the center of the park, and a Catholic priest was preparing to offer Holy Communion. Rabbis and Protestant ministers were also on hand to participate.

The center of attention was a small man bundled in a hooded parka. He was seated on a chair in front of the altar with his wife and children. Though only 41 years old, he had needed 2 men to help him to his seat. His supporters, seeing his weakness and his gauntness, were deeply concerned for his life. The man was Cesar Chavez, leader of the farm workers' union, and he had not eaten for 25 days.

Two farm workers help a weakened Chavez take his seat at the mass on March 10. During his fast, Chavez's weight plunged from 175 to 140 pounds, and supporters feared for his life. Chavez, however, maintained that his physical suffering helped focus his mind on spiritual values.

Why had Chavez willfully placed himself near death? Why had he steadfastly refused to touch food while his weight plunged from 175 to 140 pounds? Even some of those who had worked with him closely were confused and disturbed. They wondered if Chavez was merely trying to call attention to himself, trying in effect to martyr himself. Others who shared Chavez's political goals but not his religious faith were put off by the mystical element of the fast and the involvement of the clergy. The grape growers, locked in a bitter struggle with the UFWOC, considered Chavez's fast nothing more than a publicity stunt designed to elicit sympathy from the American public. But those who knew Chavez best—those who had worked with him to build a union from the ground up—knew that everything he did was directed toward a single purpose: to better the lot of the American farm worker.

The farm workers had begun their strike in 1965, refusing to labor in the vineyards of California's grape growers. Though farm workers had struck in the past, few of the strikes had ever been successful: The growers, with the local politicians and the police on their side, had almost always beaten down the strikers. Chavez, the son of migrant workers, knew this history well. He was totally committed to the philosophy of nonviolence, which had been applied successfully in the Deep South by black civil rights activists. As the leader of the farm workers, Chavez was determined to use these tactics against the grape growers. He saw no other way to win the strike. "If we had used violence," he told the writer Peter Matthiessen, "we would have won contracts long ago, but they wouldn't be lasting, because we wouldn't have won respect."

Chavez emphasized his belief in nonviolence at many union meetings, but he may have expressed himself most eloquently in a letter to the American Farm Bureau Federation, a growers' association: "If to build our union required the deliberate taking of life, either the life of a grower or his child or the life of a farm worker or his child then I would choose not to see the union built. . . . We hate the agribusiness system that seeks to keep us enslaved, and we shall overcome and change it not by retaliation or bloodshed, but by a determined nonviolent struggle carried on by those masses of farm workers who intend to be free and human."

Chavez's approach yielded dramatic results. The picketing of the fields, a nationwide boycott of California grapes, and skillful use of the mass media won the farm workers the sympathy of the nation and pressured several large growers into signing contracts with the union. But the growers were a tenacious group who had never before given in to a union. They fought back with threats, violence, court orders, and maneuvers such as using different labels on their boxes to evade the boycott. With pressures on the union mounting, it became harder and harder for Chavez to restrain those members of his union who wanted to destroy the growers' property or beat up strikebreakers. As the violence began to break out, he knew he had to put an end to it. As Chavez described it to journalist Jacques Levy several years later: "I thought I had to bring the Movement to a halt, to do something that would force them and me to deal with the whole question of violence and ourselves. We had to stop long enough to take account of what we were doing. . . . So I stopped eating."

Chavez stopped eating on February 14 and announced his decision to the membership four days later. Then he went to the union headquarters for the duration of the fast. He spent most of his time in bed to conserve his energy, otherwise conducting the business of the union as usual. Every night a mass was held on the grounds outside the building, highlighting the religious element of penitence in Chavez's fast. To Chavez himself, the mass also served as a means of organizing. People traveled as far as 70 or 80 miles to see him, perhaps 10,000 people in all during the 25 days. Chavez used the opportunity to explain what he was doing, to emphasize

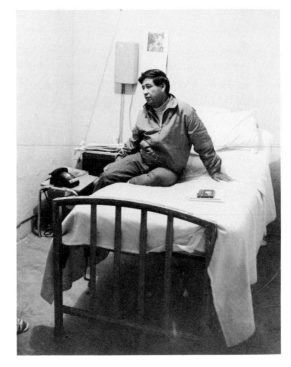

Chavez conducted his fast from a hospital bed in his modest office at the union headquarters in Delano, California. As many as 10,000 people visited Chavez during the fast; he used the opportunity to talk about the farm workers' struggle and to garner support for his union.

the importance of the farm workers' struggle for justice and the necessity for nonviolence.

Chavez's physical suffering was considerable at first. "In the beginning I had nightmares about food," he recalled, "about eating chicken or good vegetables. Then I would wake up to find I hadn't eaten anything. . . . Then I went through the hunger pains, the headaches, cleaning myself out." After a week, however, the physical pain subsided, and Chavez found himself in a state of heightened awareness in which he could remember conversations word for word. He began to see his mission more clearly and to distinguish things that were truly important from those that were less important. After two weeks, the pain returned, afflicting Chavez's legs and his chronically bad back. "I think that because of a lack of calcium, I began to draw calcium from my bones. The pains in my joints were horrible."

But Chavez persevered, and his efforts had their desired result. The entire nation was aware of what he was doing and what his reasons were. Union members came to the headquarters and swore that they would never use violence, if only Chavez would begin to eat. In one instance that Chavez remembered with amusement, a worker who had had too much to drink entered the room, pinned Chavez down, and tried to force a taco into his mouth. Weak as he was, Chavez struggled successfully until a group of union members pulled the worker off. The man was in serious danger until Chavez got out of bed and convinced his supporters that the poor fellow had been acting out of genuine concern and had meant no harm.

Finally, on March 10, at the urging of his doctor, Chavez ended his fast. On the flatbed truck, he prepared to receive bread from the Reverend C. Wayne Hartmire, one of the many local clergy who supported the farm workers' cause. It was an emotional moment for the farm workers, intensified still more by the presence of Senator Robert F. Kennedy of New York. Kennedy, having heard that Chavez was ending his fast, had chartered a plane in Los Angeles and arrived in Delano to be present. The crowd was so enthused at the sight of him that he could barely make his way to the flatbed without being swept off his feet. Five years after the assassination of his brother President John F. Kennedy, Robert Kennedy was considering a bid for the presidency in the 1968 election. He had gained a reputation as a champion of America's poor and had come out in favor of the farm workers' struggle in Delano as early as 1966. During the fast, Kennedy had sent Chavez a telegram of support. Now he had come to take part in the Holy Communion, in this case by means of the *semita*, or poor man's bread, in accordance with the Mexican ritual.

In front of the television cameras, Kennedy gave Cesar Chavez a piece of bread. Then, in the Boston accent which his brother had made familiar to the nation years before, he delivered a simple message: "The world must know that the migrant farm worker, the Mexican American, is coming into his own right."

Following Kennedy, Paul Schrade of the United Auto Workers union presented the farm workers with a check for $50,000 to be used for the completion of the UFWOC headquarters at Forty Acres, a plot of land on the outskirts of Delano where Chavez had conducted his fast. It was a measure of how much acceptance the UFWOC, begun in 1962 on Chavez's meager savings of $1,200, had gained from the labor movement.

The next to speak was the Reverend Jim Drake. He had been a friend and ally of Chavez's from the very beginning of the union struggle. Drake read a speech that Cesar Chavez had penned earlier that day:

"Our struggle is not easy. Those who oppose our cause are rich and powerful, and they have many allies in high places.

"We are poor. Our allies are few. But we have something the rich do not own.

"We have our own bodies and spirits and [the] justice of our cause as our weapons.

"When we are honest with ourselves, we must admit that our lives are all that really belong to us. So it is how we use our lives that

Paul Schrade, regional director of the powerful United Auto Workers union, was one labor leader who supported Chavez's fledgling National Farm Workers Association (NFWA). At the March 10 mass, Schrade presented the NFWA with a $50,000 contribution from the auto workers.

determines what kind of men we are. It is my deepest belief that only by giving our lives do we find life.

"I am convinced that the truest act of courage, the strongest act of manliness, is to sacrifice ourselves for others in a totally non-violent struggle for justice. To be a man is to suffer for others. God help us to be men!"

Before the end of 1968, both Robert Kennedy and the Reverend Martin Luther King, Jr., the nonviolent leader of the civil rights movement, would be struck down by assassins' bullets. As Peter Matthiessen wrote, "There was a growing fear among the poor that all their champions were to be assassinated." Threats had been made against Chavez, and his supporters constantly feared for his life. Chavez agreed to take precautions, but he was not overly concerned about his safety. "Death is not enough to stop you," he said. "You're really too busy to think of it. Unimportant, day-to-day things get your attention, which is just as well." Concentrating on the daily struggle, Chavez survived and went on with his work. That was what life had prepared him to do from the start.

A Mexican village on the Rio Grande. During the 1880s, Cesario Chavez, Cesar Chavez's grandfather, crossed the Rio Grande into Texas. By working on the railroad and in the fields, he saved enough money to bring his wife and 14 children to the United States.

CHAPTER TWO

Sal Si Puedes

Cesar Estrada Chavez was born on March 31, 1927, on a farm near Yuma, Arizona. His family had originally come from the northern Mexican state of Chihuahua. Chavez's grandfather Cesario had been a virtual slave on a big ranch known as the Hacienda del Carmen, but he had escaped across the Rio Grande to El Paso, Texas. In El Paso, Cesario Chavez worked on the railroad and in the fields. By 1888, he had saved enough money to send for his wife and 14 children. Reunited, the family worked hard and prospered. In time, they moved to Arizona and settled in the North Gila Valley, along the Colorado River in the Arizona desert. They dug irrigation ditches on the land and homesteaded more than 100 acres that spread along the valley floor at the foot of the dry hills.

By 1924, all the Chavez children had married and established their own homes, except for Librado (whose name means "the freed one" in Spanish). When he was 38, Librado married Juana Estrada and continued to work on his parents' farm. Librado was a handsome, powerfully built man and a hard worker. In addition to his farm chores, he bought a business located on the valley floor below the family ranch. The business consisted of three separate buildings—a store with living quarters above it, a garage, and a pool hall with a small counter where sodas, cigarettes, and candy were sold.

Cesar Chavez was born above the store, the second of six children. He and his younger brother Richard were lively and mischievous, and among other things they became expert pool players. Librado Chavez was usually too busy to give the boys much supervision. That task fell to Juana Chavez, who had a powerful influence on Cesar's thoughts and future career. She was a deeply religious person who believed it her Christian duty to help the poor. Often, she would send Cesar and Richard out to find a wandering tramp and invite him home for a meal. Juana Chavez always had on hand many Spanish *dichos*, or sayings, most of them stressing

Juana and Librado Chavez, Cesar Chavez's parents, during the 1940s. They raised six children in Arizona's North Gila Valley and worked long hours to provide for them. In addition to helping out on his father's ranch, Librado Chavez operated a store and a pool hall.

Cesar Chavez and his sister Rita on the occasion of their First Communion. Chavez adopted his mother's strong religious faith and was guided by her two main principles: the duty to help the poor and to turn the other cheek when attacked.

the themes of charity and nonviolence. "She would always talk about not fighting," Chavez later recalled. "Despite a culture where you're not a man if you don't fight back, she would say, 'No, it's best to turn the other cheek. God gave you senses like eyes and mind and tongue, and you can get out of anything.' She would say, 'It takes two to fight.' That was her favorite. 'It takes two to fight, and one can't do it alone.' When I was young I didn't realize the wisdom in her words, but it has been proved to me so many times since."

When the Great Depression gripped the country after the stock market crash of 1929, Librado Chavez, like so many other Americans, lost his business and was forced to move his family back into his father's adobe ranch house, where his mother now lived alone. Here the family attempted to live by farming, but this too proved impossible. In addition to the crippled economy, the Southwest was struck by severe drought. Without sufficient water from the Colorado River to fill the irrigation ditches, the land became a virtual desert. The once-fertile soil in which Librado Chavez had planted corn, squash, chili, and watermelon was now cracked clay. Without any crops to market, the family was unable to pay the taxes due on the land. Finally, in 1937, the state stepped in and seized the property.

In August 1938, Librado Chavez left the farm and went to look for work in California. He found a job threshing beans in Oxnard, in the southern part of the state, and sent for the family. They lived in a small shack in a crowded neighborhood, and after the harvest season returned to Arizona. The Chavezes had hoped to raise enough money to reclaim their land, but the following year it was sold at public auction. The trees the children had played under were uprooted; the dry ditches that had been filled with cool water were filled in by bulldozers; the corrals that had once held the family's horses were torn down. Finally, the Chavezes had to pack their belongings and themselves into an old Studebaker and head out for good to California. They were no different from the 300,000 other Americans who had lost their land to depression and drought and were now condemned to the life of the migrant worker.

To be a migrant agricultural worker is to perpetually search for work; to search for another job that will help feed the family one more day, one more week. Day by day, the struggle for survival accumulates into months, then years, then becomes a lifetime of working and searching for the next job, the next field where the whole family will work together, walking the long field rows, kneeling to pick certain crops, climbing ladders to pick others.

It is a life of movement. And because of the constant movement and the low pay, the children have to help. When the children help, there are times that they will not be able to attend school, and so the process perpetuates itself. Another child in the fields, another one out of school who will be unable to find something other than field work later. And those who do attend school experience only parts of a school year. A child may go to one school while certain crops are picked and move to other schools in other towns as the time to pick a new crop arrives. It becomes a routine—packing and moving, searching for work, studying lessons repeatedly because of the variations in school curricula, or not being exposed to certain studies at all. By the time the children are grown,

The children of migrant workers shared their parents' hardships. They often had to work in the fields and were rarely able to attend school on a regular basis. Cesar Chavez was only able to complete the seventh grade before he had to quit school entirely and help support his family.

they are left with a mental patchwork of education that they will always be uncertain about, if they ever have time to worry about it at all.

For the migrants, the search for work is a matter of gathering information. A worker listens to others talking about where to go next, what crops they plan to pick. One listens for names of farms and farmers, truckers and foremen and seeks them out.

But there have always been unscrupulous people among those who provide information. Growers can hire touts, people who scour the countryside in search of migrants and tell them that there is work at a particular farm, that the homes there are beautiful and cheap, that there is much money to be made. Of course, when too many migrants arrive in one place, the growers can exploit them by keeping wages low.

Librado Chavez heard that there were peas to pick in Atascadero, California, just north of San Luis Obispo. And so the Chavez family traveled there, packed into two separate cars. But when they arrived, they learned that the work had been over for three weeks. And so they drove around until someone they met mentioned another site, 100 miles north, in Gonzales. There, the Chavezes crowded into a single room above a bar. At night, the jukebox downstairs would blare music into the room, keeping everyone awake. During the day, Librado Chavez went around town looking for work.

He met a recruiter who was being paid $20 for each family he sent to Half Moon Bay. The recruiter promised a specific wage, but when the family arrived, the wage was only half that. Too many workers were competing for the jobs.

The first time they picked peas, the Chavezes got another education. It took two hours to fill one hamper, walking along the rows bent over at the waist. They carried the baskets full of peas to the end of the fields for sorting and weighing. The workers were paid only for those considered "good peas." In 3 hours, the Chavez family—all of them combined—had made 20 cents.

When a week had passed, they heard about another job. Again, "there was good money to be made," this time in San Jose, just south of San Francisco. Along with many others, the family quickly packed and moved. But with so many people arriving at the same time, and everyone in the same desperate condition, San Jose would be no different.

In San Jose, the Chavezes came to a barrio, or Spanish-speaking neighborhood, that was clustered between two unpaved dead-end streets and surrounded by fields and pastures. The houses, tightly crammed together and separated now and then by tall unpainted fences, were little more than shacks with backyard privies. Most of all, there were people: a multitude, packed into each house and each lot. The name of the barrio was Sal Si Puedes—Get Out If You Can.

As Chavez later recalled, "When we first arrived in Sal Si Puedes, our problem was getting in, not out." The barrio was so packed with humanity that the Chavezes could find nothing better than a single room in a lodging house. The room measured 10 feet by 12 feet, and 11 people had to sleep in it.

During the day, the search for work continued. The farmers were paying one-and-a-half cents a pound for picking cherries, if one could get a job. Earlier, the pay had been two cents a pound. But now there were too many workers, and the price had gone down.

When the cherry harvest ended, work began in the apricot orchards. After harvesting the fruit, the workers would stand at long wooden tables in the packing sheds, cutting each apricot neatly all around, removing the pit, and placing the pitted fruit on long, six-foot wooden trays. The apricots would then be sprinkled with sulfur and dried on the trays. A family doing this work would average about 30 cents a day.

After the apricot season, a lull would come before the next planting. But the families would wait. It would be more expensive to move and risk finding nothing than to stay where they were. The prune season would soon arrive. After the prune season was over, many would travel down to Oxnard, their battered cars snaking in long lines down the California roads. In Oxnard, they would pick walnuts. The workers would shake the nuts loose from the trees with long rough poles with metal hooks. It was a backbreaking job, but the harder part, for some, was picking the nuts off the ground, one by one, bent over at the waist for hour after hour.

For the Chavez family, the winter after the walnut harvest was the low point. For the first time, they had nowhere to live. Eventually, a woman working beside them in the walnut orchards offered them her yard. Cesar, Richard, and their cousin Manuel could sleep in the open, and the rest would sleep inside an eight-foot-long tent. In the summer, this might have been an adventure. But in the winter, when the Pacific fog rolled into Oxnard, the cold, damp air would seep through everyone's clothes, even those inside the tent. Eventually, Cesar's shoes disintegrated from the dampness, and he had to go to school barefoot through the mud. "After school," he recalled, "we fished in the canal and cut wild mustard greens— otherwise we would have starved."

Like many young people around him, Cesar Chavez saw his parents age with each season in the fields. It was even more difficult when his father suffered a chest injury in an automobile accident in 1942. After that, Cesar dropped out of school. He was 15, but he had not gone past the seventh grade. Like many dropouts, he thought at the time that he would work to help his parents and then go on to high school in a year or two. But that was not the way things turned out.

Instead, the years of field work blurred into one another, as did the crops. In the winter, Cesar thinned lettuce and sugar beets, ensuring that the plants were not too close together. He did this job with a short-handled hoe, bending over all the time and using his hands when the plants were too small to be hoed without destroying them all. "Every time I see lettuce," he remarked years later, "that's the first thing I think of, some human being had to thin it. And it's just like being nailed to a cross."

When other work was scarce, there were onions. Bending over as he walked across the field, Chavez would poke his fingers into the earth and plant the onion seedlings four inches apart, "just like dealing cards—one, two, three, four—no rest, just walking fast, bent over, to push the plants in. . . . Some farms had good land, which was lucky, but others had bullheads, little thorny things that punctured our fingers. It hurt, but we couldn't stop. We had to make that acre."

Acre by acre, Cesar used up another 2 years of his youth; one day, he realized that he was 17 years old and had still not returned

Farm workers use short-handled hoes to thin young plants, ensuring that each has room to grow. A grueling task, the job demands that laborers move slowly up and down long rows, constantly bent over at the waist as they work. Chavez frequently thinned beets and lettuce as a young man.

to school. He liked the adult responsibility of helping his family, but he had seen with his own eyes that very few farm workers held on to their strength much past the age of 35.

In 1944, in the midst of World War II, Cesar Chavez enlisted in the U.S. Navy and served for two years as a deckhand on a troop transport. He had signed up only to avoid being drafted into the army on his 18th birthday, and he recalled his navy service as the worst two years of his life — "this regimentation, this super authority that somehow somebody has the right to move you around like a piece of equipment. . . . And there was lots of discrimination."

Growing up, Chavez had experienced discrimination in many forms: schoolteachers who considered Mexican-American children mentally backward, restaurants that refused to serve anyone with dark skin, farmers who treated their workers as little more than beasts of burden. Finally, while on a weekend leave in Delano, California (later to be the scene of his greatest triumph as a labor leader), he decided not to put up with it anymore. He made a point of sitting in the section of a movie theater reserved for whites; when asked to move to the section reserved for Mexicans, blacks, and Filipinos, he refused. The police came and took him to jail. There was nothing the police could charge him with, so they let him go with a warning. He was angry, but for the moment, he recalled, "I didn't know then how to proceed." It would take time before he learned to channel his anger into social activism.

For the time being, he went back to the fields and began a family of his own. When he was 15 and traveling with his family in search of work, the Chavezes had stayed for a time in a tent city outside Delano. Cesar went into town to look around and ended up in a malt shop called La Baratita. There, he met a group of young people and was drawn to a girl his own age wearing flowers in her hair. He learned that her name was Helen Fabela and that she worked in the People's grocery store. Cesar became a constant visitor to the store, and he and Helen began to date. They married in l948; using Librado Chavez's old Studebaker and some money that Cesar had saved, the newlyweds spent their two-week honeymoon touring the old Spanish missions scattered throughout California.

After their honeymoon, the Chavezes returned to Delano, where Cesar picked grapes in the summer and cotton in the winter. At their home, a one-room shack, the new Chavez family had no electricity or running water. It was cold, so they kept the little kerosene camping stove on day and night. They had no car of their own, so Cesar Chavez would hitch rides back and forth to work when the fields were located at a distance.

When they got tired of being on their own, Cesar and Helen moved to San Jose, where Cesar's brother Richard was working on an apricot farm. Cesar would work one or two days a week when his brother could find an opening for him. The rest of the time, he looked for a more permanent job. Helen had by now given birth to the first of the couple's children, Fernando. Seven more were to follow.

The whole Chavez clan was reunited in Greenfield, near San Jose, where they rented a small farm and tried growing strawberries. But after two years of constant work, including Christmas, they had made nothing for themselves and decided to give it up. Cesar ended up picking string beans for $1 to $1.50 an hour while Helen gave birth to 2 more children. Finally, Cesar and Richard found work handling lumber in Crescent City, 400 miles to the north. Once they got used to the unfamiliar work, they were able to send for their families. After a year and a half, they grew tired of the rainy northern California weather and returned to San Jose, where Richard began work as a carpenter and Cesar found a job in another lumber mill. After a childhood of roaming the state of California, they had finally escaped from the fields. For many that might have been success enough. But Cesar Chavez had already seen that there were bigger things to fight for.

Cesar Chavez (second from right) began to work as an organizer for the Community Service Organization (CSO) in 1952 and became general director in 1958. After the CSO board of directors repeatedly refused to back his efforts to create a labor union for farm workers, Chavez quit his comfortable job in 1962 and struck out on his own.

CHAPTER THREE

Organizing

Cesar Chavez had his first direct experience with the labor movement in 1948, when he was 21 years old. He and his family were picking cotton near Wasco, in the San Joaquin Valley in central California, when a caravan of cars drove by. The people in the cars were waving flags out the windows, urging the workers in the fields to strike. Through loudspeakers they cried that wages were too low. But the loudspeakers were blaring so loudly that it was hard to understand the words. Some of the workers in the field put their hands up to their ears, to let the people in the cars know that they could not hear.

The Chavez family understood well enough. They had already taken part in spontaneous walkouts when they felt that some injustice was being done. In Wasco itself, some time before, they had heard another worker complaining to the foreman that his sack of cotton was not being correctly weighed and that he was being short-changed. The two men argued, and Librado Chavez joined in to support his fellow worker. When the foreman refused to give in, both the aggrieved worker and the Chavezes walked off the job.

The sight of other workers in their cars, waving flags and shouting, *"Huelga! Huelga!"*—the Spanish word for "strike"—inspired the Chavezes to stop working and join the caravan. They rode through the San Joaquin Valley, yelling to the workers hunched over in the fields. That night, the strikers held a rally in the town of Corcoran. Many workers came to express their support, but after a few days the strike fizzled out, and everything went back to normal.

This particular strike had been organized by the National Farm Labor Union. While Cesar was growing up, Librado Chavez had belonged to a number of different unions: the Tobacco Workers, the Cannery Workers, the Packinghouse Workers. Cesar himself had not joined, but he read the papers and kept himself informed on the major events and leading personalities in the labor movement.

Besides his father, another important influence on Cesar Chavez during these years was Father Donald McDonnell, a young Catholic priest who came to Sal Si Puedes, where there was no Catholic church, to conduct masses for the Mexican Americans. Chavez, who had inherited his mother's religious faith, helped the priest in his work. It soon became apparent that Father McDonnell was interested not only in the souls of his parishioners but also in their material well-being. "We had a long talk about farm workers," Chavez recalled. "I knew a lot about the work, but I didn't know anything about the economics, and I learned quite a bit from him. . . . He had a picture of a worker's shanty and a picture of a grower's mansion; a picture of a labor camp and a picture of a high-priced building in San Francisco owned by the same grower. . . . Everything he said was aimed at ways to solve the injustice."

Father McDonnell introduced Chavez to transcripts of congressional hearings on agricultural problems and to biographies of St. Francis of Assisi, the 13th-century monk who dedicated himself to the service of the poor, and of Mohandas K. Gandhi, who by nonviolent means had led India's struggle for independence from the British Empire after World War II. The example and teaching of Gandhi and St. Francis reinforced what Chavez had learned from his mother. His first steps as an organizer, however, came from a man named Fred Ross, whom Chavez also met in Sal Si Puedes and of whom he later said quite simply: "He changed my life."

Ross, a tall, lean man with a deeply lined face, was born in San Francisco in 1910. He graduated from the University of Southern California in 1936. Though he had hopes of becoming a teacher, there were no such jobs available in the midst of the depression, so he became a social worker with the state relief administration. Later, he worked with the Farm Security Administration, a government agency set up under President Franklin D. Roosevelt's New Deal. Ross's main job was to give out essential commodities, such as flour and beans, to those in dire need. But this was not enough for Ross. Sent somewhere to do a survey, he instead began to organize the poor to do something about what was happening around them. Saul Alinsky, a Chicago-based community organizer who had created the Industrial Areas Foundation, heard about Ross and offered him a job in September 1947. Alinsky wanted Ross to organize Mexican Americans in Los Angeles, the center of the Mexican-American population. From Los Angeles, Ross's organizational activities branched out to other California barrios. In June 1952, Ross found himself in Sal Si Puedes, looking for Cesar Chavez.

But Chavez had no interest in meeting Ross. He was sure that Ross was just another *gringo* (a derogatory term used by Mexicans to describe white North Americans) who wanted something from the Mexicans. He was accustomed to sociologists coming to the barrio with their notebooks, studying poor people as though they were animals in a laboratory, and he had no use for such intruders. Having been warned that Ross was coming, Chavez went across the street to his brother's house and told Helen to give the stranger some excuse and get rid of him. The first three times, Helen covered for her husband. But when Ross came back a fourth time,

Helen got tired of making up stories. She stepped outside and pointed across the street to Richard Chavez's house. Cesar Chavez now had no choice but to hear what Ross had to say.

Ross wanted Chavez to hold an organizing meeting at his house as soon as possible. Chavez agreed, intending to give Ross a hard time and get rid of him once and for all. Chavez invited some rough characters from the barrio to the meeting, provided them with beer, and hatched a plan: When he switched his cigarette from his right hand to his left hand, the others would start an argument with Ross and throw him out of the house.

But on the night of the meeting, June 9, 1952, Ross did not ask foolish questions about what it was like to be Mexican or poor or a farm worker. Instead, he spoke quietly about the problems of the people in the area. For example, he knew that the creek right behind Sal Si Puedes carried the waste from a nearby packing-house. The children played in the water, and the sores they developed attested to its contamination. Ross wanted people to organize and get the authorities to correct such conditions. He described the outfit he had created, the Community Service Organization (CSO), and explained how his group could help the poor to empower themselves in their community.

Some of Chavez's friends still wanted to give Ross a hard time, but Chavez hustled them out of the house. Ross's words had had a deep effect on him. Up until then, Chavez had seen no alternative but to attack the problems of the poor on an individual basis. Ross had given him the idea that something could be done for the community as a whole, by the people themselves. "He did such a good job of explaining how poor people could build power that I could even taste it, I could *feel* it," Chavez later told Peter Matthies-sen. "I thought, Gee, it's like digging a hole, there's nothing complicated about it."

After the meeting, Chavez walked Ross to his car, still absorbing ideas. When he learned that Ross had another meeting on tap, Chavez jumped in the car and went along. At the end of the

CSO organizer Hiram Samaniego (left) and Fred Ross (right) recruit Chavez as a community organizer in 1952. At their first meeting, Ross immediately recognized Chavez's ability and remained a constant friend and adviser. Chavez said of Ross: "He changed my life."

evening, he agreed to meet Ross the following night in order to take part in a voter registration drive.

Ross himself was deeply impressed by Chavez's intelligence and enthusiasm. He kept a diary in those days, and when he got home that night he made a simple entry: "I think I've found the guy I'm looking for."

Chavez proved to be a diligent recruit. After working all day in the lumber yard, he went out canvassing 85 nights in a row, knocking on doors and telling people how important it was that they register to vote. By the 1952 general election, the CSO had registered 6,000 new voters. At the polls, however, the deputy registrars challenged many of the new voters, asking them to prove that they were American citizens and that they could read and write. Many of the people were offended or confused and walked away without voting.

After the election, the CSO sent a telegram of protest to U.S. attorney general J. Howard McGrath. They accused the deputy registrars, supposedly nonpartisan but all members of the Republican party, of harassing the newly registered Mexican-American voters, who would have been likely to vote for the

Democrats, generally more sympathetic to the poor. However, a number of people on the CSO board were afraid to sign the wire. They held government jobs and did not want to offend the Republicans. Chavez, however, had no hesitation about putting his name down, and this won him respect and recognition in the community.

Chavez also spent his time helping people to become citizens and conducting classes at a local school. Many people just needed to talk to him about day-to-day problems. Some were illiterate and needed someone to write a letter for them. Others spoke English poorly or not at all and needed an interpreter to accompany them to a government office. Still others needed help in dealing with the police. While addressing all these problems, Chavez organized small meetings similar to the meeting Ross had held at his house. The CSO method was to hold house meetings for three months, followed by a larger meeting at which local officers were elected. Eventually, a working CSO chapter would be set up, and the organizers would move to a new area. Through this type of organizing, more and more people in the San Jose area got to know Chavez and to respect his abilities.

When the lumber yard where Chavez worked began to lay off workers, Ross convinced Saul Alinsky, whose Industrial Areas Foundation was funding the CSO, to hire Chavez as an organizer. Chavez started in DeCoto (now Union City) and later moved north to Oakland.

Oakland was a big city, and Chavez got lost when he drove around it. His first house meeting had been set up by Father Gerald Cox, a local priest, but Father Cox was not able to attend. Chavez, who was only 25 and looked younger, was afraid that people would not take him seriously. He drove around the block several times before he had the courage to stop at the house where the meeting was to be held. When he did go in, instead of introducing himself he went and sat in a corner as though he were just another member of the group. The 10 people who had come to the meeting sat around for a while, making small talk. After 15 or 20 minutes had

Saul Alinsky, a self-described radical, ran the Industrial Areas Foundation, the CSO's parent organization. Alinsky hired Chavez as an organizer and considered him the best worker the CSO ever had. However, the two men disagreed completely about the need for a farm workers' union.

passed, one of the women wondered aloud where the organizer was. At that point, Chavez had to speak up and identify himself. "She looked at me and said 'Umph!'" Chavez recalled. "I could see what she meant, a snotty kid, a kid organizer, you're kidding!"

As he began to speak, Chavez was still unsure of himself. He explained what the CSO was all about and how important it was to organize. But he felt that his words were clumsy and disjointed. He was painfully aware that the other people in the room were older than he was and more experienced in life. Why should they listen to him? Nevertheless, by the end of the evening several people had committed themselves to organizing more meetings. "Probably they felt sorry for me more than anything else," Chavez reflected.

Following Ross's approach, Chavez continued to hold house meetings for about three months before he scheduled his first general meeting, which was to be held in the social hall of St. Mary's Church. The meeting was scheduled to begin at 7:00 P.M. At 4:00, Chavez had convinced himself that no one was going to show up. By 7:00, only 20 people were in the hall. But when the meeting was over, 368 people had come. This was Chavez's first major success as an organizer.

He called Ross to report the good news. Ross was pleased, but he did not plan to let Chavez rest on his laurels. Before long, Ross had assigned Chavez to work in Madera, in the San Joaquin Valley, and had raised his pay to $58 a week. This seemed like a lot of money to Chavez, who promptly packed his family into the car and took off for his new assignment. After Madera, there was Bakersfield, then Hanford, then other cities and towns, with never more than four months in one place. "Everywhere there were problems," Chavez recalled. "There were fights, there were countless cases where we could help people. But no matter what happened, I learned."

In 1958, Chavez was sent to Oxnard, where he and his family had once spent a cold, damp winter huddled in a tent. Chavez was sure that he knew what he had to do. A general election was coming up, and Mexican-American voters needed to be involved. A voter registration drive was the answer.

But the people of the barrios, though they came to register, did not talk much about the election. They talked instead about the jobs they were losing to the *braceros*, migrant workers from Mexico.

Mexican farmhands, known as braceros, were brought into the United States by growers to work the fields, often in violation of the law. The growers preferred to use braceros rather than local workers because the braceros were easier to exploit: They were desperate for work and had no legal rights.

According to federal law, growers were allowed to hire braceros to work in the United States—but only when no local workers were available. The workers who came to see Chavez were angry and confused. How could the growers be allowed to import braceros when there were local people actively looking for work? It was illegal, and yet the braceros were there in the fields.

Chavez started by applying for work himself at one of the labor camps. The people in charge told him he needed to register at the Farm Placement Service office, eight miles away. He went to register, and by the time he got back they told him that there were no more jobs to be had that day. Braceros had been turning up since 4:30 A.M., and by 6:00 A.M. all the jobs had been filled. The Farm Placement Service opened at 8:00 A.M.

On the following day, at 4:00 A.M., Chavez showed up at the labor camp with the slip from the Farm Placement Service referring him for work. He was rejected again, on the grounds that the slip had been issued the day before; it was no longer valid. In this way the growers had caught the workers in a vicious circle. There was no way a worker could get a valid referral slip in time to get a job, and the growers could claim that when the braceros turned up at the fields, no local workers had been available.

The growers were happy with this system, because they could easily exploit the braceros, who were usually trucked across the border in large numbers. Not being citizens, they had almost no rights and could be sent back to Mexico at any time. As long as they were in the United States, they had to pay for their housing and food whether they worked or not. By the time they left, many of them had nothing to take back home.

On January 15, 1959, about 1,500 workers held a rally to protest the hiring policies of the growers. The workers distributed leaflets all over Oxnard accusing the Farm Placement Service, a state agency, of acting in collusion with the growers. The following morning, Chavez and his associates called the governor's office but got no response. They then called Alan Cranston, the state controller, who had previously been sympathetic to the concerns of Mexican Americans. Cranston told John Carr, the head of the Department of Employment, to get in touch with Chavez. Carr referred Chavez to another official and then proceeded to duck him for the next month.

Chavez went on the offensive. He approached other workers and asked them to fill out applications at the Farm Placement Service. The workers laughed because they were convinced it was useless. But Chavez coaxed them into it. "What have we got to lose?" he said. "Let's go along for the ride." One young worker agreed to come, and more followed. Chavez made copies of the applications and the referral cards. After a month, he was able to present John Carr with documentary proof that registered workers were consistently being denied jobs. Carr got Farm Placement Service officials to meet with the CSO, and eventually the growers hired three local workers. That was a small enough token, but after only a few hours on the job the workers were fired on the pretext that they lacked experience. One man had been working in the fields for 17 years.

The CSO then began to picket the bracero camps at night. When the people who ran the Farm Placement Service left their office at the end of the day, they were confronted by CSO demonstrators shouting, "We want jobs!" Chavez's people handed out leaflets to Oxnard merchants, indicating that local people could not shop in their stores because the braceros were getting all the work and taking the money back to Mexico. In this way, Chavez was developing the techniques he would use on a national scale as a union leader.

Chavez was further encouraged by the support he received from a U.S. Department of Labor official who was called in to monitor the situation. Speaking privately, the official told Chavez that the last thing his opponents wanted was adverse publicity. Several days later, Chavez organized a march on the Farm Placement Service. The workers registered several times each, so that they could obtain a pile of referral cards. Then 60 or 70 men, followed by a caravan of cars carrying women and children, marched to the Jones Ranch, one of the main employers of braceros.

Chavez had seen to it that the news media were informed, and when the marchers reached the ranch, police officers and television crews were out in force. Chavez climbed up onto a car and made a speech. He said that there was no longer any point in registering for work because the system was a farce. At this point he set his referral card on fire, and the other workers followed suit. Soon there was a big pile of cards going up in flames. "The TV cameras just ate it up," Chavez recalled.

Despite the publicity gained by the march, the growers refused to give in. But after another month went by, the U.S. secretary of labor, James Mitchell, visited the area to make a speech to a business group. The CSO picketed the hall where Mitchell was speaking and then staged a march in Oxnard that was attended, in Chavez's recollection, by as many as 10,000 people. The marchers massed behind a banner bearing the image of the Virgin of Guadalupe, the patron saint of Mexican field workers, and sang Mexican hymns. The police protested that the marchers had no permit for a parade, but confronted by 10,000 people, they were powerless to intervene. "That's when I discovered the power of the march," Chavez said.

As federal officials got more and more involved, state officials increased their pressure on the Farm Placement Service until the agency agreed to cooperate fully with the CSO. The growers finally began to use the CSO office as a hiring hall, coming to pick up the workers that the CSO selected and paying them the wage that the CSO set. After a 13-month struggle, during which he had often worked from 5:00 A.M. to 10:00 P.M. and had seen his weight dwindle from 152 to 127 pounds, Chavez had won his first great victory as an organizer of farm workers.

Chavez began his farm workers' union in 1962 with no steady income and only $1,200 in the bank. He admitted later that he was frightened at first. But his fear vanished when he saw that he and his family could survive without his paycheck.

CHAPTER FOUR

La Causa

Fresh from his victory in Oxnard, Cesar Chavez felt that the time to build a union had come. The CSO, however, would not approve such a project. Instead, the CSO board appointed Chavez national director and transferred him to Los Angeles. Financially, it was a big step up for Chavez. He and Helen now had 8 children, and the salary of $150 a week, plus expenses, would enable them to make ends meet without a problem. Nevertheless, Chavez fretted in Los Angeles. "More than anything else, I wanted to help farm workers," he later said.

Six months later, when Chavez returned to Oxnard, he found that all his work there had gone for naught. The braceros were back in the fields, and the local people were out of work. Without a strong organization backing the workers, the growers had gained the upper hand again. Chavez was furious, but at that point there was nothing he could do to change the situation.

Chavez spent two more years as national director of the CSO, trying all the time to convince the leadership to let him create a farm workers' union. His efforts were fruitless. Saul Alinsky considered Chavez the best worker he had ever employed, but Alinsky did not have Chavez's intimate attachment to the soil and the people who worked it. Alinsky was convinced that the farm workers' best hope was to acquire the political and technical skills that would enable them to prosper in the urban society of the future. Chavez was obsessed with liberating the people who were currently toiling in the fields. In the end, there was nothing left for Chavez to do but resign from the CSO and form a union on his own.

It was a move he had carefully discussed with his wife, Helen. "The more we talked about it, the more I organized her," he recalled. "I saw the trap most people get themselves into—tying themselves into a job for security. It was easier for us and our family to try to escape poverty than to change the conditions that keep so many workers poor. But we inherited the poverty from our fathers and our fathers from our grandfathers and our grandfathers from their fathers. We had to stop someplace!"

Helen agreed to go along with the union idea for 10 years, and Chavez quit his job, with a total of $1,200 in the bank. "At first I was frightened, very frightened," he later confessed. "But by the time I had missed the fourth paycheck and found things were still going, that the moon was still there and the sky and the flowers, I began to laugh. I really began to feel free."

The Chavezes went back to Delano, Helen's hometown, where they could at least count on the support of Helen's family if they were desperately in need. In every other way they were starting from scratch. Although the AFL-CIO, the most powerful labor organization in the United States, had set up the Agricultural Workers Organizing Committee (AWOC) in 1959, Chavez did not want to be restricted by the political pressures that affected the activities of large unions. While still with the CSO, he had been offered as much as $200 a week to work for AWOC and turned it down. "I can't organize with you guys," he told them simply. "You're not going to give me the freedom I need."

Cesar and Helen Chavez, pictured here with seven of their eight children, returned to Delano, Helen's hometown, when Cesar quit his job with the CSO. Helen Chavez often worked long hours in the fields to make ends meet, and the children helped their father distribute leaflets up and down the San Joaquin Valley.

As soon as Chavez got to Delano, he drew a map of all the towns and farming camps in the San Joaquin Valley, 86 locations in all, and determined to visit each one of them. His purpose was to recruit workers into his new union, the National Farm Workers Association (NFWA).

The Reverend Jim Drake, who became one of Chavez's principal allies, was highly skeptical of the NFWA's chances: "I really thought Cesar was crazy. Everybody did except Helen. They had so many children and so little to eat, and that old 1953 Mercury station wagon gobbled up gas and oil. Everything he wanted to do seemed impossible. He used his tiny garage as his headquarters, but it was so hot in there, all the ink melted down in the mimeograph machine I lent him."

Anyone who had studied the history of agricultural labor unions in California, as Chavez had, was aware that farm workers had never achieved any lasting success. Beginning in the 1870s, when farmers had discovered the fertility of the California fields, waves of immigrants had worked the land. The Chinese came first, then the Japanese, then the Mexicans, even Hindus from India.

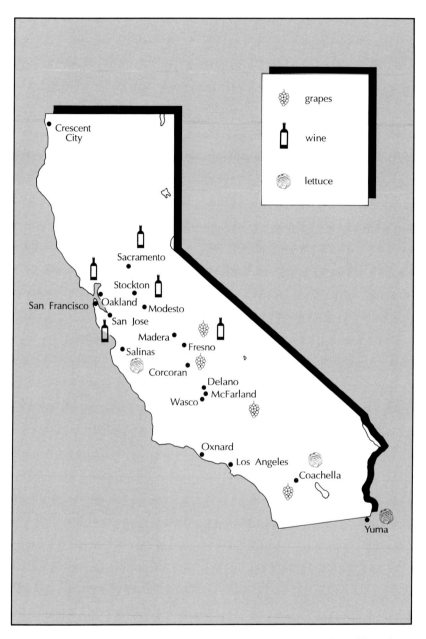

This map of California shows the cities that figured most prominently in Chavez's early life and later career. Symbols indicate major areas producing grapes, wine, and lettuce.

The growers had learned how to play off one group against the others, using their need for work and racial antagonisms to keep wages low. When workers did organize, the growers and the local authorities combined to crush their unions, jailing the leaders and forming vigilante groups to beat and terrorize organizers.

Even in the New Deal years, when Congress enacted legislation protecting workers' rights, the federal government had been no help. The all-important National Labor Relations Act, passed in 1935, specifically excluded farm workers from its protective provisions, on the grounds that they were not engaged in interstate commerce. In the years following, the agriculture industry had beaten back attempts to amend the law.

Chavez was determined to succeed where others had failed. His plan was simple: He would drive from town to town in his old station wagon and talk to the workers. No mass meetings at first, just quiet conversations. Often he took his young son Anthony (known as "Birdy") with him, because Helen was working in the fields and there was no money to pay a baby-sitter. While his father drove, Birdy slept on the front seat. When Chavez came to a place he had targeted and saw some workers in the fields, he would drive up as close as he could and then get out. With Birdy toddling through the field rows beside him, Chavez would ask the workers about conditions on the job. As he got to know them better, he made it clear that he was there to help them with any problems they had. If a worker had a hearing with the labor commission or an appointment to try for compensation for a work-related injury, Chavez would go along. And while the worker drove, Chavez would talk. Sometimes he would not even talk about the job or the union, just establish human contact and personal trust. "All he did for three days was make me laugh," marveled one man, who nevertheless came out of those three days as a convert to the union cause.

Chavez was not afraid to describe himself as a fanatic. "You must stay with one thing and just hammer away, hammer away, and it will happen," he said. That was the way he recruited his closest aides in the union. He convinced Dolores Huerta to give up her job with the CSO and become an organizer with the NFWA, where the pay was five dollars a week plus room and board. Then he went after his cousin Manuel, who was making $1,500 a month selling cars in Yuma, Arizona—quite a handsome income in 1962. Manuel Chavez had no intention of giving up his comfortable life-style in order to return to poverty. But Cesar kept hammering away at him, reminding Manuel of the tent in Oxnard and all the other hardships the Chavezes had endured together. Did they not have an obligation to help those who were still suffering? Finally, Manuel agreed to come to California for six months and give organizing a try. He never went back.

Even the Chavez children were recruited into La Causa (the Cause), as the union came to be called by the farm workers. On Fridays, when the children came out of school, Chavez would load them into the car, and they would hand out leaflets throughout Kern, Kings, Tulare, and Fresno counties. In the summer, they would work late into the evening and right on through Saturday and Sunday.

The children began to treat it as a game. When their father stopped the car, they went tearing off through the streets. After a while, the other children in the barrio would come running out to join in. In this way, the whole barrio might be covered with leaflets in 15 or 20 minutes. Then the Chavez children would hop back in the car, and off they would go to the next stop.

Responses to the leaflets were slow to come—there might be one every two or three days. When he got two letters in one day, Chavez was ecstatic. He would answer each letter and then go to see the people in person. "The growers didn't know he was in town," Jim Drake recalled, "but the workers knew. After a while, they were coming to his house day and night for help. . . . The pains taken by Cesar were never part of an act. They were a very real extension of his philosophy that human beings are subjects to be taken seriously."

By the fall of 1962, enough workers had joined the NFWA to justify holding a convention. The meeting took place on September 30, in an abandoned theater in Fresno.

Manuel Chavez had gone to Fresno ahead of time to make the arrangements. He carried a card identifying him as secretary-treasurer of the union, but he had no money. Ever the resourceful organizer, Manuel spoke to the owner of the theater and said he wanted to rent the place for a meeting. The theater owner asked for $50. Manuel explained that the president of the union was flying in with the money and would pay as soon as he arrived. After the theater owner agreed to wait, Manuel went next door to a grocery and got bologna sandwiches and Cokes for all the delegates, also on credit. As soon as the delegates arrived, Manuel told them what he had done, and they all reached into their pockets to make a contribution. In the end, there was enough money to pay for the rent of the hall and the food, with a bit left over. The union's first convention could then begin.

The first order of business was the unveiling of the union flag. Ever since the march in Oxnard behind the banner of the Virgin of Guadalupe, Cesar Chavez had been convinced that the farm workers' movement needed a unifying symbol. He wanted something that was striking enough to be easily recognized at a distance. It would also have to be simple in its design so that the workers could make the flag on their own.

Chavez and his aides came up with a design patterned on the red-and-black flags traditionally used by striking workers in Mexico. As their symbol, they adopted the eagle, the sacred bird of the Aztecs, the Indian people who had ruled Mexico before the Spanish conquest in the 16th century. The NFWA eagle would be solid black, the wings drawn with straight lines so that anyone could make a reasonable facsimile. The eagle was displayed on a white circle, and the rest of the flag was deep red.

Chavez had a huge flag made up, 16 by 24 feet. Before the convention began, he and his aides stretched it over the screen of the movie theater and covered it with paper. When the delegates were all in their seats, Manuel Chavez tore the paper away and revealed the flag. There was a collective gasp from the audience. Everyone was impressed, but not everyone was pleased. Some saw the red flag as the symbol of communism; others were reminded of the Nazi flag adopted by Germany during Hitler's Third Reich; still others objected to the color scheme, suggesting that a gold eagle on a blue background would have been more pleasing.

Chavez responded to the criticism by telling the delegates that the flag signified whatever one wanted it to signify. "To me it looks like a strong, beautiful sign of hope," he asserted. Manuel defended the flag in more vigorous terms: He said that the black eagle represented the dark situation of the workers; the white stood for hope; and the red background symbolized the struggle and sacrifice the workers would have to make to build their union. "When that damn eagle flies," he concluded, "the problems of the farm workers will be solved!"

Some delegates were so upset by the flag that they left the union for good. The 150 who remained got down to the business of electing officers and adopting a constitution. They also decided on a motto: Viva La Causa (Long Live the Cause). Union dues were set at $3.50 a month. This was not a small sum to a farm worker, but Manuel Chavez convinced his cousin Cesar that if the workers did not have to make a sacrifice to belong to the union they would not put in the effort to make it a success.

The first weeks after the convention were a struggle. Two hundred workers had signed up to pay dues, but after 90 days had passed, all but 12 had dropped out. The recruiting started all over again, sometimes with the aid of fiestas and barbecues that attracted as many as 1,000 people. In one instance, Manuel Chavez

The red-white-and-black NFWA flag was unveiled at the union's first convention, in 1962. Some delegates thought the flag represented communism, others nazism. Chavez defended the design, saying, "To me, it looks like a strong, beautiful sign of hope."

recruited a new member and collected his $3.50. When he called the office 3 days later to report his success, they knew all about the new member—the man's wife had just died, and the union had to pay him $500 under its death-benefit program.

Despite all these setbacks, Chavez and his aides found that once they got a person to pay dues steadily for six months, they had a solid member who would never desert the union. They ended their first year in a spirit of optimism. "We gave ourselves three years of hard work," Chavez remembered. "If we couldn't do it in three years, then we couldn't do it. But we made a firm promise among ourselves that if we couldn't do it, we'd never blame the people, we'd blame ourselves."

No one had to accept any blame, because three years later the NFWA and Cesar Chavez were engaged in a labor struggle that aroused the conscience of the nation.

Dolores Huerta defiantly holds up a sign reading Huelga, *the Spanish word for "strike." The NFWA began its strike against California's grape growers in 1965 and fought for five years before gaining a final settlement.*

CHAPTER FIVE

Huelga

In 1966, the writer John Gregory Dunne visited one of the major ranches near Delano, California, to see how grapes were grown and picked. "The workers hunch under the vines like ducks," he wrote. "There is no air, making the intense heat all but unbearable. Gnats and bugs swarm out from under the leaves. Some workers wear face masks; others, handkerchiefs knotted around their heads to catch the sweat."

When Cesar Chavez came on the scene in 1965, these workers were earning as little as a dollar an hour for their toil. (The average annual income of a farm worker at this time was $1,500, while the federal poverty level was set at $3,000). On many ranches, there were no toilets in the fields. The growers usually provided drinking water (no one could have withstood the 100-degree heat without it) but often charged the workers for what they drank and forced them to share a rusty tin cup. As if the lack of sanitary facilities were not injurious enough to their health, the workers were also exposed to the lethal chemicals that the growers sprayed on the crops to kill insect pests.

Union organizers found the grape pickers a prime target because grapes require cultivation 10 months out of the year. Thus the grape workers were a more stable force than other agricultural workers who migrated from harvest to harvest. They also earned more money than the average migrant and tended to be more interested in further improving their lot. In addition, the law permitting the use of braceros had expired in 1964, thus stabilizing the work force. The AFL-CIO's agricultural workers union, AWOC, had sent Larry Itliong, a native of the Philippines, to organize his fellow Filipinos working on the Delano grape farms. On September 7, 1965, the AWOC workers went on strike.

When the growers began to recruit workers of other nationalities, predominantly Mexicans, to break the strike, Itliong went to Cesar Chavez and asked for his help. Chavez did not feel that his own union, the NFWA, was ready to get involved in a strike. For one thing, the union had a total of $100 in its strike fund. But Chavez feared that if he avoided this challenge, the organization

In 1965, grape workers earned as little as $1 an hour, toiling in 100-degree heat under unsanitary conditions. By the mid-1980s, after 20 years of labor struggles, the workers represented by Chavez's union were up to $7 an hour, plus medical and retirement benefits.

might never recover. He called for a strike vote, and on September 16, Mexican Independence Day, the membership of the NFWA voted unanimously to join the Filipinos on the picket line.

John Gregory Dunne interviewed Wendy Goepel, one of the first volunteers to join the union cause, and recorded her recollection of the strike's beginning:

> I'll never forget that first morning. . . . We all got to the office at 3:30 A.M. and just waited for people to show up. We were all very nervous. We didn't know if they would. It was like that moment at the beginning of a party when the host and hostess wonder if anyone will come, if they got the date right, or if the invitations were sent out. But then they began to filter in, and Cesar went around telling them if they had a gun or a knife or anything sharp to leave it behind.

Chavez's warning served notice that this strike was going to be different from any that had gone before. It was not only that Chavez personally abhorred violence. He explained to the writer Peter Matthiessen that the rejection of force could actually be a source of power: "If you have a gun and they do too, then you can be frightened because it becomes a question of who gets shot first. But if you have no gun and they have one, then—well, the guy with the gun has a lot harder decision to make than you have. You're just—well, *there*, and it's up to him to do something."

As a shrewd organizer and a student of labor history, Chavez understood that the NFWA, which was now called upon to lead the strike, could not beat the growers by a head-on assault. They did not have the money, and they did not have the physical power. If they tried to flex their muscles, the strike would end up the way others had in the past—workers jailed and beaten, leaders arrested or driven out of town by vigilantes. Chavez knew that along with the courage of his people his greatest asset could be the conscience of the American public.

Chavez calculated correctly. In 1965, the United States was indeed ready to hear the farm workers' appeal. The self-satisfaction of the 1950s had already begun to wear thin by 1960, when John F. Kennedy based his campaign for the presidency on the concept of a New Frontier. He appealed to the desire of Americans, particularly the young, to eradicate the injustices still rampant in the nation's social system.

Much of the population had achieved prosperity during the post–World War II era. Industrial workers, who had barely survived during the depression of the 1930s, now often enjoyed a life-style previously reserved for businessmen. However, many Americans had been excluded from the feast. In 1960, U.S. government studies revealed that 40 million Americans—22 percent of the population—were living below the poverty line.

Blacks in the South had been denied not only economic opportunity but their basic rights as citizens; residents of Appalachia, a mountainous region stretching down the eastern seaboard, often lived their entire life without plumbing or electricity; and migrant workers all over the country were suffering under conditions that most people associated with the 19th century.

In response, civil rights leaders such as the Reverend Martin Luther King, Jr., had been attacking racial segregation in the South. Politicians such as Kennedy were calling for massive government aid to Appalachia. And on November 25, 1960, the day after Thanksgiving, CBS had aired a television documentary entitled "Harvest of Shame." Narrated by the nation's leading television commentator, Edward R. Murrow, "Harvest of Shame" presented in graphic images and interviews the hardships of migrant fruit pickers in Florida. All at once, Americans were forced to confront the idea that the men and women who picked their fruits and vegetables were often little better off than slaves. Chavez meant to turn that knowledge into a weapon.

On the first day of the strike, 1,200 workers joined in, affecting an area covering 400 square miles of vineyards. They formed picket lines along the roads bordering the fields. The strikers walked back and forth, holding signs bearing the black eagle of the NFWA above the word *Huelga*—"Strike." As they marched, the strikers urged those working in the fields to come out and join them.

In many cases, the growers reacted violently. At one farm, the grower pointed a shotgun at the strikers and threatened to kill them. He grabbed their pickets signs, set them on fire, and when they did not burn fast enough to suit him, he blasted the signs with his shotgun. Some growers would walk along the picket line, kneeing and elbowing the strikers or knocking them to the ground. In other cases, growers ran their trucks and tractors through the edges of the fields, covering the pickets with dust and dirt.

In Delano itself, the police were watching the NFWA's tiny office at First and Albany streets. Each time someone left, the police would follow, sometimes questioning the workers as to what they were doing. The police also began to photograph the people on the picket line and fill out reports on each striker.

The union's response to the growers and the police was to remain nonviolent and make a show of cooperation. Every time Chavez himself was photographed by the police he took as much of their time as possible, making sure that they spelled everything correctly in their report and asking questions about every part of the procedure—sometimes, he was able to stretch this out for an hour. In addition, groups of workers would sometimes get up in the middle of the night and drive around the fields, forcing the police to work around the clock.

Very quickly, Chavez began to broaden the base of the strike. He arranged for a group of 44 strikers to get themselves arrested for shouting "Huelga!" on the picket line, and the next day he spoke to a big rally at the University of California in Berkeley. The Berkeley students were politically active and had just launched their Free Speech Movement, demanding a say in the running of the university. Explaining that the arrested pickets had been fighting for their own right of free speech, Chavez asked the students to donate their lunch money to the strike fund. From Berkeley he went on to Mills College and San Francisco State with the same message. By the end of the day, the union had collected $6,700 in dollar bills.

In addition to appealing for funds, Chavez encouraged people to volunteer. He wanted people from different backgrounds and did not care what their political views were as long as they were devoted to La Causa. He later remarked: "If we were nothing but farm workers in the Union now, just Mexican farm workers, we'd only have about 30 percent of all the ideas that we have. There would be no cross-fertilization, no growing. It's beautiful to work with other groups, other ideas, and other customs. It's like the wood is laminated."

Chavez was particularly eager to bring in volunteers from such civil rights groups as the Congress of Racial Equality (CORE) and the Student Nonviolent Coordinating Committee (SNCC). These men and women had organized sit-ins and protest marches in the South, and they had learned to respond nonviolently to every form of assault and intimidation. They were the ideal instructors for the inexperienced troops of the NFWA.

Perhaps the union's most powerful step—certainly the move that focused national attention on the grape strike—was the decision to boycott the grapes of major growers. It also gave the labor movement a taste of Chavez's toughness.

NFWA members began to picket the docks where cargoes of grapes were about to be shipped abroad. In response, the International Longshoremen's and Warehousemen's Union (ILWU) refused to load grapes on the waiting ships. This gratified the farm workers but annoyed many established labor leaders, who did not like to see old-line unions forced to strike on behalf of some upstart group. They pressured Al Green, the head of AWOC, to put some heat on Chavez.

Green did his best to persuade Chavez to take his pickets off the docks. When Chavez refused, Green angrily threatened to take all his support away and break the NFWA. "He was so angry, he cussed me," Chavez told journalist Jacques Levy, "and I cussed him back. . . . 'Don't you ever threaten me,' I said. 'You're not big enough to threaten me, and you're not even big enough to begin to carry out your threats.'" Green backed off. The pickets stayed, and the grapes sat on the docks.

In November 1965, the NFWA refined its boycott tactics further. Instead of going after all the growers at once, they would concentrate on a single target. The union chose Schenley Industries, Inc., which had 3,350 acres under cultivation in Delano. Schenley was especially vulnerable because only a fraction of the company's $500 million in annual sales derived from farming. The bulk of the revenue came from wine and liquor. The union reasoned that a national boycott of Schenley's brands would get results. The company would not want its whole operation jeopardized by such a relatively small component as the grape farm and would be eager to settle with the NFWA, thus setting an example for the other growers.

John Gregory Dunne described the launching of the operation:

> From an atlas, Chavez picked thirteen major cities across the United States as boycott centers, and then raised a boycott staff, all under twenty-five, from workers and volunteers who had impressed him on the picket line. They left Delano penniless and then hitchhiked or rode the rails to the various cities where they were to set up shop. Chavez gave the boycott staff no money, both out of necessity and to prove a theory. He reasoned that if a person could not put his hands on enough money to maintain himself on a subsistence level, then he would be of little use raising money for the boycott and setting up an organization. In most cities, boycott staffers went to union locals and begged room, board, an office, a telephone, and whatever help was available. Across the country, they recruited some 10,000 people to pass out leaflets or to telephone neighbors, friends, churches, and stores, urging support of the boycott.

Supporters of the farm workers demonstrate outside a New York City supermarket. The NFWA grape boycott was organized in cities across the United States by volunteers who handed out leaflets and marched on picket lines, urging shoppers to shun California grapes.

The growers continued to insist that their workers were happy and that Chavez had little support. Many accused him of being a Communist. Nevertheless, the boycott was gaining national attention, NFWA membership was climbing, and organized labor was embracing the farm workers' cause. In December 1965, the AFL-CIO officially endorsed the grape strike at its annual convention; the following day, Walter Reuther, president of the powerful United Auto Workers, made a special trip to Delano in order to present a check for $5,000 and pledge his total support. At this point, the strike was costing $40,000 a month, and without contributions of money, food, clothing, and other necessities—both from other unions and from ordinary citizens—the NFWA would have found it difficult to carry on effectively.

The NFWA's final step in achieving national prominence came in March 1966, when the U.S. Senate Subcommittee on Migratory Labor came to Delano in order to conduct an investigation of the grape strike. The subcommittee was chaired by Senator Harrison Williams of New Jersey, a staunch ally of the farm workers, but its most prominent member was Robert F. Kennedy. At this point in his career, Kennedy was regarded by some as merely an ambitious politician without any deep commitment to social issues. He was not sure that he wanted to attend the hearings at all and skipped the first day; then he took the advice of an aide and went to Delano. What he heard there converted him to the farm workers' cause.

At one point in the hearings, Kennedy asked Leroy Gaylen, the local sheriff, why he had arrested a group of pickets who were being theatened by strikebreakers. The sheriff replied that he had wanted to avoid trouble. When asked why he had the strange idea of arresting the potential victims instead of the people making the threats, Gaylen replied that he thought it better just to remove the cause of the problem. When Senator Williams announced a lunch break, Kennedy remarked acidly, "Can I suggest that in the interim period of time . . . that the sheriff and the district attorney read the Constitution of the United States?"

Walter Reuther (center), president of the United Auto Workers, came to Delano in 1966 to show his union's support for the striking NFWA. The strike was costing $40,000 a month, and the NFWA could not have carried on without donations of money and food from established unions and the general public.

Before he left Delano, Kennedy made it clear that he supported the union unconditionally. If the NFWA needed any further boost in the regard of the American public, this association with the Kennedy mystique did the trick. Kennedy and Chavez forged a personal bond that lasted until the senator's death and even beyond.

The day after the hearings, the NFWA decided to tackle the state of California. The state legislature had passed a law guaranteeing companies such as Schenley a minimum price for their liquor but had done nothing, in the eyes of the union, to guarantee farm workers a decent wage. For that reason, the strikers were going to march 250 miles to Sacramento, the state capital, to present their case to the governor. The marchers planned to be on the road for 25 days, arriving in Sacramento on Easter Sunday.

The religious symbolism of the arrival date was quite intentional. Chavez had discovered the almost mystical power of the march during his days in Oxnard, when the workers had marched with candles, singing hymns, and he meant to put this power to full use.

Sixty-seven union members began the march from the main street of Delano. The police tried to stop them from moving through town but had to give in when the marchers indicated that they were willing to wait a year if they had to, but they were not turning back. And so the workers moved out through Delano and into the San Joaquin Valley, walking single file behind the American flag, the flag of Mexico, and the banner of the Virgin of Guadalupe. Many of the marchers had their own homemade flags bearing the black eagle of the NFWA or simply the word *Huelga*.

The marchers covered 21 miles on the first day, reaching the town of Duroc. They slept where they could. Chavez had been too busy to find shoes that fit him well, and by the end of the day he had a swollen ankle and a huge blister on one foot. To emphasize the elements of penitence and endurance in the march, Chavez refused to take any painkillers. By the second day, his right leg was

In March 1966, striking farm workers march 250 miles from Delano to the California state capital, Sacramento, in order to gain support from state officials. Between the flags of the United States and Mexico they carried the banner of the Virgin of Guadalupe, the patron saint of Mexico's farm laborers.

swollen to the knee, and after a week of marching he was so ill that he had to ride in a station wagon.

Despite his pain, Chavez had to be gratified by the reception the marchers were receiving. Whenever they reached a town, the local people would come out to greet them, often in a festive mood with guitars and accordions, and the union would hold a rally in the local park. The marchers would explain their objectives and distribute copies of the Schenley boycott pledge: "I will not buy Schenley products for the duration of the Delano farm workers' strike. Get with it, Schenley, and negotiate. Recognize the National Farm Workers Association."

By the ninth day of the march, Chavez was feeling well enough to walk with the use of a cane, and he pushed on. The march had drawn so much coverage in the press that with each stop the reception was greater. In Fresno, for example, the mayor held a luncheon for the marchers and assigned half a dozen plainclothes police officers to get Chavez's people whatever they needed. In

Modesto, William Kircher of the AFL-CIO arranged a display of support from other unions. In Stockton, 5,000 people came out to greet the marchers.

Even more important, Chavez received a phone call in Stockton. The call was from Sidney Korshak of Schenley, who said that the company was ready to sign an agreement with the union. Chavez, not believing the call was legitimate, hung up the phone. Korshak called again, and again Chavez hung up. When Korshak called a third time, Chavez was finally convinced. He got into a car at 1:00 A.M. and promptly fell asleep in the backseat while the Reverend Chris Hartmire drove down to Los Angeles for the meeting with Schenley.

When Chavez reached Korshak's opulent home in Beverly Hills, Bill Kircher and other AFL-CIO officials were on hand. They all intended to sign the agreement with Schenley. Chavez let Korshak and the others know that unless Schenley signed exclusively with the NFWA, the boycott would continue. The AFL-CIO people tried to work on Chavez, but they got nowhere. "You must be kidding," he remembered telling them. "You're trying to tell me to give you a contract, when we fought for it, bled for it, and sweat for it. You must be out of your mind!"

Finally, Bill Kircher, who had fought for the farm workers in the past, came up with a compromise: The NFWA would sign the contract, and Kircher would sign as a witness on behalf of the AFL-CIO. The agreement was drawn up and duly signed. Schenley recognized the union, agreed to a union-run hiring hall, awarded an immediate pay raise of 35 cents an hour, and set up automatic contributions to the NFWA credit union. With the agreement sewn up, Chavez got back in the car and drove north to rejoin the marchers.

It was raining on Easter Sunday when the marchers finally entered Sacramento, but 10,000 people were on hand to greet them. Only 50 of the 67 who had begun in Delano had made it to the end, and these *originales* were almost lost in the press of

On Easter Sunday, 1966, 10,000 people greeted the NFWA marchers in Sacramento. Addressing the jubilant crowd, Chavez announced that the union had reached a settlement with Schenley Industries, providing the first contract for farm workers in American history.

people who, eager to be associated with the dramatic event, had joined the march for the final leg. (The union organizers made sure, however, that the *originales* held center stage on the platform at the final rally.) The union had asked Governor Edmund G. "Pat" Brown to meet with them when they arrived, but Brown was under heavy pressure from the growers and decided to go away for the weekend. Undaunted, the marchers and their supporters gathered at the state capitol building.

And there, standing on the capitol steps, Chavez was able to announce the historic agreement with Schenley. With the exception of an agreement signed in Hawaii on behalf of pineapple workers, the Schenley contract was the first ever negotiated in the history of American farm labor. It had been won by a union that had started out 4 years earlier with 1 member and $1,200.

Organized labor in New York shows its support of the grape strike in 1969.
By the end of the 1960s, the NFWA boycott had spread throughout North
America and beyond. In Europe, for example, unionized stevedores refused
to unload California grapes from incoming ships.

CHAPTER SIX

Victory in Delano

When he returned to Delano with the Schenley contract in his pocket, Chavez was under no illusion that the other growers were going to fall into line. The union would have to battle them just as hard as it had battled Schenley. The next logical target was the DiGiorgio Corporation, whose Sierra Vista Ranch in Delano covered 4,400 acres. Like Schenley, DiGiorgio relied on farming for only a fraction of its income; the bulk of it came from the marketing of such nationally known food brands as White Rose and S & W. DiGiorgio should, therefore, be equally vulnerable to a nationwide boycott.

But DiGiorgio differed from Schenley in one important way. The company had a history of breaking strikes, by any means necessary. In 1939, 1947, and 1960, for example, DiGiorgio had used political influence to obtain court orders against picketing and had then brought in strikebreakers to work in the fields. During these struggles, strikers were evicted from their work camps, beaten by law officers or vigilantes, and even packed into cars and run out of the county.

Undaunted, the NFWA began its picketing of the Sierra Vista Ranch and its national boycott of DiGiorgio three days after celebrating the Schenley contract. The boycott was immediately effective. As Chavez explained, "There were a lot of people who had fought DiGiorgio in the thirties and the forties and the fifties who started coming out of the woodwork to take them on in Chicago, San Francisco, New York."

The company quickly agreed to negotiate with the union about work rules and the procedures for holding an election on union representation. But Chavez broke off the talks immediately when he learned that two NFWA pickets had been threatened and then beaten by armed guards at Sierra Vista. "I'll be damned if I'm going to negotiate with you guys while you're beating and jailing our people!" he told DiGiorgio.

DiGiorgio got Chavez back to the table by disarming the guards, and they negotiated in such apparent good faith that Chavez was persuaded to lift the boycott. He quickly realized that he had made a mistake—the company had something up its sleeve. DiGiorgio was willing to hold elections in the fields because they expected the elections to be won not by the NFWA but by the Teamsters.

The Teamsters Union, representing workers in transport and other industries, was one of the most powerful in the United States. It was also one of the most corrupt. Under the leadership of Dave Beck and his successor Jimmy Hoffa, the union had been accused repeatedly—in congressional hearings, in the courts, and in the press—of misusing its members' pension funds and of employing powerful gangsters to help it organize and control certain industries. (In 1966, Beck was in prison; Hoffa later served a jail sentence as well and vanished in 1975, presumably the victim of a gangland slaying.) The Teamsters were such an embarrassment

Jimmy Hoffa led the Teamsters Union from 1958 to 1967, when he went to prison for bribery, mail fraud, and misuse of union pension funds. During Hoffa's heyday, the Teamsters began to compete with the NFWA for the right to represent California's farm workers.

to the labor movement that in 1957 the AFL-CIO decided to expel them from its ranks.

As an independent union with a thirst for power, the Teamsters were all the more inclined to extend their influence. In exchange for recognition (and more union dues rolling into their coffers), they were prepared to offer the growers what are known as sweetheart contracts—agreements that benefit the company more than the workers. The Teamsters had already demonstrated this practice in California. In 1961, a strike of lettuce workers against Bud Antle, Inc., had been broken when Antle signed a contract with the Teamsters. A year later, the company obtained a million-dollar loan from the Teamsters pension fund. Chavez knew all about these dealings, and as he ruefully remarked, "DiGiorgio knew it, too."

DiGiorgio did not rely solely on the Teamsters for help. As it had in the past, the company went to court and on May 20, 1966, obtained an injunction against picketing. The injunction enabled DiGiorgio to send recruiters down to Texas and Mexico and bring back busloads of strikebreakers, without any fear that union pickets would turn away the new workers. As a finishing touch, the company required the new workers to sign authorization cards for the Teamsters.

Saul Alinsky, Chavez's former boss, told John Gregory Dunne that Chavez should have gone the company one better and cut his own deal with the Teamsters: "I would have gotten a patron, . . . someone who can lean on the growers. I would have gone to Hoffa. I would have said, 'Listen, everyone thinks you're nothing but a goddamn hoodlum. You need to pretty yourself up. And the way to do it is to help the poor migrant Mexican. You do it and people won't call you Hoodlum Hoffa anymore. They'll be calling you *Huelga* Hoffa.'"

Whether or not Alinsky was completely serious, Chavez was not very likely to abandon everything he believed in. Instead, he called a union meeting and asked for suggestions. No one had any, other than the idea that it was time to use violence, which was

Helen Chavez fully supported her husband's plan to start a farm workers' union. "I never had any doubts that he would succeed," she later said. However, with eight children to raise and bills to pay, Helen Chavez did not often have time to march on union picket lines.

emphatically rejected by the membership. Shortly after the meeting, however, three women came to see Chavez with a proposal that was typical of the NFWA. They knew they could no longer picket in front of DiGiorgio's gates, but would it be all right if they held a mass there?

Chavez was immediately inspired. "I got Richard [Chavez] and had him take my old station wagon and build a little chapel on it. It was like a shrine with a picture of Our Lady of Guadalupe, some candles, and some flowers. We worked on it until about 2:00 in the morning. Then we parked it across from the DiGiorgio gate where we started a vigil that lasted at least two months. People were there day and night."

At first only union members attended, but gradually the new workers from the camps began to sneak out and come to the prayer vigils. When they did so, the strikers were able to explain the union cause and get them to sign authorization cards for the NFWA. "It was a beautiful demonstration of the power of nonviolence," Chavez asserted.

The tide began to turn in favor of the union. On June 16, Judge Leonard Ginsburg declared DiGiorgio's antipicketing injunction invalid. At the same time, the Mexican-American Political Association, at the urging of the NFWA's Dolores Huerta, was pressuring Governor Brown to help the farm workers. At last, after more persuasion by the AFL-CIO's Bill Kircher, Brown appointed an independent arbitrator to rule on the validity of the union election at DiGiorgio. The arbitrator, Dr. Ronald Haughton of Wayne State University in Michigan, recommended a set of rules for the election and scheduled it for August 30.

In order to gain support for this decisive contest with the Teamsters, the NFWA realized that it would finally have to enter into a formal alliance with the AFL-CIO. For this reason, Chavez agreed to merge the NFWA with AWOC. The new union was to be known as the United Farm Workers Organizing Committee (UFWOC). The merger upset some of the NFWA's more radical

William Kircher, director of organization for the AFL-CIO, appears with Dolores Huerta at a U.S. Senate hearing in Washington, D.C. Kircher backed the NFWA from the beginning of the grape strike; in 1969, the union joined the AFL-CIO and became the United Farm Workers Organizing Committee (UFWOC).

supporters, who had no use for the old-line unions. But the majority of the membership realized that the farm workers could not confront the Teamsters without solid backing.

The merger required some changes. The AWOC organizers had been earning $125 a week, whereas Chavez's people were still getting $5 a week plus room and board. Almost all the AWOC organizers quit, with the exception of the stalwart Larry Itliong. A few had to be forced out. "One guy had a Cadillac," Chavez recalled. "I said, 'You're not going to organize with me with a damn Cadillac! You either get rid of the Cadillac or leave the Union.' So he left the Union."

Some of the benefits of belonging to the AFL-CIO became immediately apparent when the Teamsters started bringing goons into Delano to intimidate the UFWOC people. In a flash, Bill Kircher got on the phone to Paul Hall, the head of the Seafarers International Union, which represented all the merchant seamen. As Kircher told the story: "I don't think there were ten hours elapsed between the time I made that phone call and into Delano drove about fourteen SIU members. You should have seen some of them! There was one black fellow who had about a twenty-two-inch waist and about a seventy-inch chest. . . . Some of the others were just as impressive, too. . . . We never had a minute's violence from the time they got there."

When the election was held, the UFWOC defeated the Teamsters, 530–331.

The victorious union took no time to rest. The leadership decided to go after Giumarra, the largest grower of table grapes. After attempting unsuccessfully for several months to negotiate an agreement, the union finally declared a strike against Giumarra on August 3, 1967. In December, another nationwide boycott was called, with the same effectiveness as the Schenley boycott. In New York City, for example, Mayor John Lindsay issued an order forbidding any city agency to purchase California grapes. But Giumarra,

The state of California set up elections in September 1969, allowing farm workers at the DiGiorgio Corporation to choose between the Teamsters and the UFWOC. Here, Chavez and his supporters are jubilant as they learn of their 530–331 victory.

like DiGiorgio, was a formidable opponent. In order to defeat the boycott, the company began using different labels on its boxes, some bought from other companies and others invented. This mislabeling was against state regulations, but the company got away with it; the tactic enabled them to get their grapes into stores that would otherwise have refused to handle them.

One year into the Giumarra strike, with the union and the company in a deadlock, Chavez began his 25-day fast. It was a time when the union's energies were at a low ebb. There appeared to be little chance of defeating the growers without violence. The fast helped to turn the tide, both by convincing the UFWOC members to support Chavez and by reaffirming the justice of the farm workers' cause. As Peter Matthiessen summed it up: "Without question, the fast worked. It taught the farm workers that Chavez was serious about nonviolence, that it wasn't just a tactic to win public support; and it taught them what nonviolence meant."

By 1969, the growers were showing definite signs of weakness. The boycott had severely affected their business; it had even spread to Europe, where unionized stevedores refused to unload California grapes from incoming ships. Because of the drop in sales, the number of growers had declined from 200 to 60 in just 5 years, and the total acreage under cultivation had declined from 13,000 to 7,500. In a lawsuit filed against the union in April, the growers claimed that the boycott had cost them $25 million in lost revenues. Finally, a group of growers from the Coachella Valley, headed by Lionel Steinberg, agreed to negotiate with the union.

The growers appeared to be ready to sign a contract, but Chavez was not satisfied with what they were offering. He was convinced that if the union kept the pressure on, the workers would come out with something much better. By taking this position, Chavez antagonized not only the growers but many of his supporters in the labor movement, in government, and in the churches, who felt that after four years of struggle, it was time to come to terms. Those four years were very much on Chavez's mind as well. As he later remarked, "Steinberg thought that because he was willing to talk to us, he was doing us a favor. . . . He forgot about those four years of badgering us, disregarding the wishes of the people, . . . putting people out of a job, and bringing in strikebreakers."

Chavez was vindicated, at least partially, when two companies that were managed and partially owned by Steinberg agreed to the union's terms: $1.75 an hour and 25 cents a box, with 10 cents an hour to be put into the union's health and welfare fund and 2 cents an hour going toward a fund for workers who lost their jobs due to age or the introduction of machinery.

Steinberg did his best to bring the other growers into line, but they were a stubborn lot when it came to unions. Many of the major growers—the Giumarras, the Dispotos, the Kovaceviches—were the sons of European immigrants who had in many cases come to the United States penniless and built their farms with years of hard work. Like their fathers, the sons were rugged individualists who simply did not want anyone telling them what they could or could not do. In Chavez, they found an opponent equally tough, equally stubborn, equally accustomed to hard work. John Gregory Dunne, visiting Delano to write about the strike, came away with this assessment of Chavez's character: "The curious thing about Cesar Chavez is that he is as little understood by those who would canonize him as by those who would condemn him. . . . The saintly virtues he had aplenty. . . . But Chavez also had the virtues of the labor leader, less applauded publicly perhaps, but no less admirable in the rough going—a will of iron, a certain deviousness, an ability to hang tough in the clinches."

In the end, Chavez's vision of change won out over the grower's passion to maintain the status quo. The boycott was relentless; all over the country, people were refusing to buy grapes unless they saw the unmistakable black eagle of the UFWOC on the box. One by one, growers began to approach the union. Chavez watched the trickle turn into a flood:

The day after [Kaharadian, a major grower] signed a contract, he sold ten thousand boxes in five hours. In three days he emptied his cold storage. Not only that, but Union grapes with our Eagle on them were selling from fifty cents to seventy-five cents more a box.

We started getting an average of five to ten calls a day from growers asking, "What do I have to do to get the bird on my grapes?"

We told them, "If you sign the contract, we'll give you the bird!" The eagle was flying.

It took until July 17, 1970, for the final break to come. On that date, 23 growers announced that they were ready to negotiate. The companies were responsible for 42 percent of all the grapes grown in California and included the union's most bitter opponents.

The negotiations took place in the Holiday Inn at Bakersfield. Despite the mediation efforts of California's Catholic bishops, it was not a simple matter to bring the two sides together after five

The black eagle of the UFWOC had become a national symbol by 1970. Because many shoppers refused to buy California grapes unless they saw the union label on the box, growers began to call the union, asking, "What do I have to do to get the bird on my grapes?"

In the Stardust Motel in Delano, Cesar Chavez and John Giumarra, Sr., sign a contract agreement on July 29, 1970, officially ending the five-year grape strike. The terms of the contract, which covered 26 major growers in the San Joaquin Valley, included wage increases and health insurance for the farm workers.

years of conflict. After a week of bickering, the Giumarras, father and son, called the union at 1:00 A.M. and said that they wanted a private meeting on the spot.

Chavez, tormented by his chronic back pains, was less than enthusiastic, but he went to the Stardust Motel in Delano to meet the Giumarras. John Giumarra, Sr., also had a bad back, and the two men began by discussing their suffering and the various treatments they had tried. Then they sat down to hammer out a settlement. The following day, the Giumarras got the growers together, and Chavez summoned his negotiating committee. After another 24 hours of wrangling over the details, both sides came to an agreement: There would be a union hiring hall, protection for the workers against pesticides, wages of $1.80 an hour (rising to $2.05 by 1972), 10 cents an hour to the Robert F. Kennedy Health and Welfare Fund, and 2 cents a box to an economic development fund.

The grape strike ended officially on July 29. The farm workers had won a tremendous victory, but they had no time to savor it. Almost immediately, they were plunged into a desperate fight for survival in the lettuce fields of Salinas.

On August 24, 1970, UFWOC lettuce workers went out on strike in Salinas, California. The union called the strike because lettuce growers were signing sweetheart contracts—agreements that benefited the employers at the expense of the workers—with the Teamsters.

CHAPTER SEVEN

Taking On the Teamsters

In July 1970, the UFWOC negotiators were enjoying some beer in the Stardust Motel in Delano, celebrating their victory in the grape strike, when someone from the union burst in with news that had just come over the radio. The Teamsters had signed 30 contracts with lettuce growers in the Salinas Valley. Journalist Jacques Levy, who was in the room, jotted in his notebook: "That ends the celebration."

The UFWOC people were angry and frightened. If the Teamsters were able to get away with their backdoor tactics, eventually every grower in California would be doing business with them at the expense of the farm workers. All the work of the UFWOC would go to waste.

Chavez was ready for the challenge. He had begun to organize the lettuce workers four years earlier, and he had always known that his union would have to have a showdown with the Teamsters sooner or later. Delano had just been a skirmish.

In addition to the Teamsters and the growers, there were powerful political forces lined up against the union. Ultraconservative Ronald Reagan had defeated Pat Brown in the 1966 gubernatorial election. Whereas Brown had tried to sit on the fence during the farm labor struggles, Reagan made it clear that his sympathies were all with the growers. It was no better on the national level. Another conservative Republican, Richard Nixon, was in the White House, and Nixon had very close ties to the Teamsters and their new president, Frank Fitzsimmons. The UFWOC could expect no real help from either the state or federal governments.

At the end of July, Chavez held a large rally in Salinas and challenged Governor Reagan, who had called for farm workers to vote on which union they wanted, to go ahead and set up elections. Then he accused the lettuce growers and the Teamsters of a "great treason against the aspirations of those men and women who have sacrificed their lives for so many years to make a few men rich in this valley. . . . It's tragic that these men have not yet come to understand that we are in a new age, a new era, that no longer can a couple of white men sit together and write the destinies of all the Chicanos and Filipino workers in this valley!"

Jacques Levy recorded the response: "The workers, massed by large crimson union banners bearing their companies' names, punctuate the meeting with cheers and cries of 'Huelga!' Their singing vibrates with militancy. The spirit of Delano flares in Salinas."

As expected, Governor Reagan evaded Chavez's offer of elections. The union had no choice but to go after the growers who had signed with the Teamsters. Once again, the work stoppage and the boycott emerged as the major weapons. It was not difficult to organize workers when the workers learned that the Teamsters had signed contracts calling for wage increases of only half a cent an hour.

A UFWOC volunteer shows a New York City subway rider where to sign her petition supporting the union's lettuce boycott. The boycott was effective, but the lettuce growers, with the Teamsters behind them, proved to be stubborn opponents.

Chavez's people also had reason to be optimistic about the effects of a boycott. As with the grape growers, some of the biggest lettuce growers were owned by major corporations that were concerned about their national image: InterHarvest was owned by the powerful United Brands Corporation, Freshpict by Purex, and Pic 'N Pac by the S. S. Pierce Company. Ironically, it turned out that Eli Black and Maury Kaplan, president and chief executive of United Brands, had both been convinced by their children to support the farm workers' boycott of California grapes. Now they were on the receiving end.

Despite these advantages, the union was squarely on the firing line. Wherever the Teamsters went there was sure to be violence, and Salinas was no exception. Jerry Cohen, the UFWOC chief attorney, was beaten by two thugs while investigating a work stoppage, and other union members were subjected to the same treatment. These strong-arm tactics were not as easy to counter as they had been in Delano, because the Teamsters were now spread out all over the Salinas Valley.

Though Chavez never worried much about his own personal safety, his aides had convinced him some time before that he at least ought to take basic precautions. His office at Forty Acres in Delano was fireproof, with 10-inch-thick walls, and he had agreed to have a guard dog with him at all times, a German shepherd named Boycott. In Salinas, Chavez used a secret office about a block away from the union headquarters. The setup was described by Jacques Levy as "a small, empty store with a tiny back room. For security reasons, the pane glass front and glass front door have been painted. No one can see in, but the filtered light accentuates the bleakness and dreariness of the surroundings, dingy walls, and a couple of battered wooden desks and chairs. The back room is all but filled by the hospital bed [used by Chavez to ease his back pain]. A heavy metal bar cradled on metal brackets lies across the back door, a substitute for a broken lock."

With these precautions in place, the union pursued its non-violent tactics, with quick results. On August 26, 1970, Chavez called for a nationwide boycott of Chiquita bananas, marketed by United Brands, the parent company of InterHarvest. The very same day, the company asked for negotiations. Within a week, the union had an agreement with InterHarvest that called for a wage increase to $2.10 an hour, considerably more than the $1.85 provided by the Teamsters contract.

The Teamsters reacted with more violence. Strikers reported being threatened with chains and baseball bats, and a number of windshields were broken by rocks. At one point InterHarvest was unable to move its trucks for nine days because the Teamsters were blocking them. By the UFWOC's reckoning, the Teamsters had at least 40 goons installed in the Towne House, a Salinas hotel. They were headed by Ted Gonsalves, who had been called in from a Teamsters local in Modesto and drove around Salinas in a luxurious black limousine.

At one point, Gonsalves lured Bill Kircher of the AFL-CIO to a room in the Towne House and surrounded the room with thugs. If he had thought of intimidating Kircher, Gonsalves had miscalculated. Kircher had taken the precaution of calling in the Seafarers again; a group of them hurried over and ran the Teamsters off. Kircher then got hold of the mayor of Salinas, the city manager, and the police chief. He told them that unless they were willing to curb the Teamsters, the AFL-CIO would close down the ports of Los Angeles and San Francisco and bring every Seafarer on the West Coast into Salinas to deal with the Teamsters. The city officials promised that there would be no more trouble and that InterHarvest would have no problem moving its trucks.

As was perhaps inevitable, the violence was not limited to one side. In September, the police arrested three UFWOC members for the shooting of a Teamster organizer in Santa Maria. The man accused of pulling the trigger had earlier been banned from a UFWOC picket line for attacking someone with a lead pipe, and Chavez held himself personally responsible. "I should have been there," he insisted. More than anyone, he realized that if the UFWOC descended to the level of the opposition, it would soon be finished.

Perhaps as a means of penance as well as a means of attracting support to the struggle, Chavez decided to put himself personally at risk. The union had been boycotting the lettuce of Bud Antle, the first company to ally itself with the Teamsters, and Antle had responded by getting a court order against the boycott. When Chavez refused to lift the boycott, he was charged with contempt of court and ordered to appear at a hearing.

The hearing took place on December 4, 1970, in Salinas. Two thousand workers poured into Salinas from all over the state in order to attend the hearing. They marched the mile from the union headquarters to the courthouse in double file, holding flags and candles, and then filled the building and the courtyard. As Jacques Levy described the scene: "They stand quietly, sometimes kneeling to pray . . . for more than three and a half hours, until the trial ends, so quiet that no one in the courtroom can tell there are two thousand farm workers in and around the building."

In the courtroom itself, the union's lawyer, Bill Carder, argued that the injunction was unconstitutional, while Antle's attorney insisted that it was valid and should be obeyed, although he emphasized that the company did not want to send Chavez to jail. When Judge Gordon Campbell took a 10-minute recess to consider his decision, Chavez had no doubt what the verdict would be. "He hates us," Chavez remarked to an aide.

When Judge Campbell returned, he began to read an opinion so long that it had obviously been written before the hearing. The upshot was that Chavez was going to jail for contempt of court; the sentence would last until he called off the boycott. The judge also imposed a fine of $10,000 but angrily reduced it when reminded by Bill Carder that the maximum fine in such cases was $500. Chavez, predictably, was undaunted. He immediately sent out the order, "Boycott the hell out of them!"

For the first three days, Chavez was miserable in jail because he wanted to be out taking part in the union struggle. Then he realized that he would never survive unless he adapted himself to the situation. He drew up a strict schedule for all his activities— reading, exercise, sleeping, answering mail, washing, meditating— and faithfully adhered to it.

Meanwhile, in a parking lot across from the jail, the farm workers set up a makeshift shrine in the back of a rented pickup truck. They made a vow to keep the vigil until Chavez was released from jail, and one man even proposed to fast for the duration.

Before he had been in jail two days, Chavez had prominent visitors. Among the first was Coretta Scott King, the widow of the Reverend Martin Luther King, Jr. King's nonviolent civil rights campaigns had clearly paved the way for the farm workers' movement, and during the Delano strike he had sent Chavez a glowing message of support. "She didn't tell me," Chavez remarked of

Two thousand farm workers poured into Salinas to attend Chavez's court hearing. Throughout the month of December, as Chavez remained in prison, the workers kept up a 24-hour vigil across the street from the jail. They erected a makeshift altar on the back of a pickup truck and held a mass every day.

Coretta King's visit, "but I could see that this reminded her of her husband being in jail. Unlike a lot of the farm worker women who came and cried, she looked at being in jail as part of the struggle."

Perhaps the most publicized event of Chavez's jail term was the visit of Ethel Kennedy, widow of Robert Kennedy. Two thousand farm workers waited to salute her across from the jail. But there were also about 200 angry antiunion and anti-Kennedy demonstrators on hand, separated from the farm workers by local police and a group of militant young Mexican Americans who called themselves the Brown Berets. The demonstrators shouted angrily as Kennedy arrived and took part in a quiet mass, all in the glare of the TV lights. Ultimately, she had to go past the pickets in order to get to the jail. A tumultuous scene ensued, with farm workers, police, and Brown Berets forging a path for the elegantly beautiful but grim-faced Kennedy while the pickets shouted and strained to get their hands on her.

Inside the jail, Kennedy spoke with Chavez for 15 minutes through a glass partition and then left quickly for the airport. Recorded in journalist Jacques Levy's notebook was Kennedy's remark to Paul Schrade, the United Auto Workers official who had set up the visit: "Paul, you throw some weird parties!"

In the midst of the publicity, the union's lawyers were working constantly to have Chavez freed. Twenty days after his conviction, the California Supreme Court ordered Chavez released pending a review of the case. He never went back: Four months later, the court ruled that Judge Campbell's injunction was unconstitutional and that the UFWOC had every right to boycott Bud Antle.

Chavez was released on Christmas Eve, and before the year was over, the Teamsters' shady dealings began to catch up with them. First, the cannery workers in Modesto learned that Ted Gonsalves

After the Teamsters pulled out of Salinas, a settlement of the lettuce strike appeared possible. However, the growers refused to negotiate seriously, and talks with the UFWOC broke off. Here, Chavez and the Reverend Jim Drake lead a rally of union supporters in New York City's Foley Square.

had used $24,000 of their union funds to fight the farm workers in Salinas, and they brought Gonsalves up on charges before the Teamsters hierarchy. Then, six men who were linked to Gonsalves and the fight against the UFWOC were indicted for transporting firearms and explosives. The Teamsters were forced to suspend Gonsalves and put the Modesto local under trusteeship while they investigated the situation.

Finally, Einar Mohn, the head of the Teamsters' West Coast operations, gave up the fight against the UFWOC. "We don't want the contracts," he told the growers. "We're out."

The way was now clear for the UFWOC to negotiate with the lettuce growers. But the growers insisted that they would not negotiate while the boycott was in place. The union called a moratorium on the boycott, and talks began. But after five months of intense negotiation, the two sides failed to make any progress. Chavez became convinced that the growers were really not serious, that they were biding their time and avoiding the boycott while they searched for a way to destroy the union. On November 10, 1971, the talks finally broke down.

While the talks were still on, agents of the U.S. Treasury Department informed the union that they had evidence of a plot to kill Chavez. According to a police informer, a group of growers in the Delano area had put out a $25,000 contract. But the prospective triggerman was arrested for another killing before he could do the job on Chavez, and the deal collapsed. Law enforcement authorities did not pursue the matter much beyond this point— the union believed the investigation was quashed by higher-ups in Sacramento and Washington—but Chavez was persuaded to go into hiding for a month.

Whatever the truth of the alleged murder plot, it served notice on Chavez and the union that no matter how many battles they won against growers and rival unions, there would always be another battle waiting.

At a news conference in Miami, Florida, in 1972, Chavez announces the first labor contract for migrant workers in Florida history. The agreement with Coca-Cola's Food Division, negotiated by Cesar Chavez's cousin Manuel Chavez, covered 1,200 citrus fruit harvesters.

CHAPTER EIGHT

New Struggles

Chavez now realized that the more success the union had, the more bitterly its opponents in business and government were going to fight back. "They know that once our Movement wins," Chavez explained, "it's going to have concrete power in terms of workers, in terms of things it can do for people. . . . And they know it's not going to stop there. They know that in a few years, farm workers will be sitting on city councils, county boards, and the courts."

The Nixon administration spearheaded the counterattack. During the latter part of the grape strike and through the lettuce boycott, the Defense Department had dramatically increased its orders from the California growers. Government officials claimed that this was a coincidence, but no one doubted that the White House was doing all it could to help the growers defeat Chavez and the farm workers. Approaching the 1972 election, Nixon and his aides stepped up their efforts to gain support from both the Teamsters and the proprietors of California's $4 billion-a-year agricultural industry.

State governments were also succumbing to pressure from the growers, and the UFWOC had to persuade state legislators to vote against laws injurious to the farm workers. Vigorous campaigns by the union in California and in Florida—where the UFWOC exposed dishonest labor contractors and publicized an outbreak of typhoid in an unsanitary labor camp—succeeded in beating back antiunion forces. The most dramatic struggle, however, took place in Arizona.

Arizona had a special meaning to the Chavez family. They had known happy times there to begin with, but then the family had been forced off their land. They had always felt that the state tax officials and the bankers had been especially eager to dispossess Mexican people of their property; Manuel Chavez in particular had always longed for an opportunity to even the score. The opportunity came in May 1972 when the Republican governor of Arizona, Jack Williams, signed an antiunion law before its legality could even be reviewed by the state attorney general. When asked about the the farm workers' objection to his hasty action, Williams replied, "As far as I'm concerned, these people do not exist."

Chavez responded to that statement by moving into the barrio in Phoenix and undertaking a 24-day fast. This one was different from the fast in Delano, in that the pain did not go away after a week. It stayed with Chavez from beginning to end. "I was miserable," he admitted later. Even more seriously, his uric acid level shot up, and his heart began to show irregularities—at one point, his doctor insisted that he enter a hospital until his condition stabilized. Despite the danger he was in, Chavez emphasized that he was fasting principally "out of a deep conviction that we can communicate to people, either those who are for us or against us, faster and more effectively spiritually than we can in any other way."

While Chavez was fasting and speaking with the many people who came to visit him, the union was busy in the political sphere. Organizers went from door to door with petitions that demanded a special election to remove Governor Williams from office. Ultimately, they collected 108,000 validated signatures, 5,000 more than were needed to mandate the recall vote. The state attorney general found a way to block the election, but the farm workers' effort paid off in the long run. So many Mexican Americans and Navajos registered to vote in the union drive that they had a major impact on the 1972 general election, placing a number of their own people in office. In 1974, they elected Raul Castro, a Democrat, as governor. "We've turned Arizona around," exulted Bill Soltero, a local union leader, acknowledging that everything had begun with Chavez's fast.

Manuel Chavez was unable to take part directly in the Arizona fight (though he led a farm workers' strike in Yuma in 1974) because he was hard at work in Florida. His organizing efforts paid off in February 1972, when the union signed a historic agreement with Coca-Cola's Food Division, covering migrant workers in the citrus groves. It was the first time migrant workers in Florida had ever enjoyed a labor contract. In the same month, the AFL-CIO decided to issue a national charter to the UFWOC, whose membership had reached 30,000. George Meany, the crusty 78-year-old president of the AFL-CIO, had always been annoyed by Chavez's independence and unconventional methods, but he was now forced to acknowledge the strength of the organization Chavez had built. Upon receipt of the charter, the union chose to be known simply as the United Farm Workers.

Support from the AFL-CIO continued to be crucial, because the UFW was still deeply embattled in California. The Salinas lettuce growers had never given in, and as of 1972 the UFW had only organized about 2,000 lettuce workers out of the possible 80,000 it had targeted. Meanwhile, the Teamsters moved in and signed contracts with 170 growers. Even the grape growers, who had made peace with the farm workers in 1970, were preparing to sign with the Teamsters when their UFW contracts expired in 1973. The UFW had no choice but to call another lettuce strike.

Chavez described the 1973 strikes as the most desperate and vicious that the union had ever engaged in. The Teamsters' thugs were out in force, without any interference from the authorities.

George Meany (center), president of the AFL-CIO, awarded an official charter to the United Farm Workers (UFW) in 1972. Chavez accepted the document from Meany in the presence of Monsignor George C. Higgins, a Catholic bishop and a longtime supporter of the farm workers' cause.

And with more injunctions granted by the courts, the pickets were the people going to jail, this time by the hundreds. After spending almost $3 million dollars of AFL-CIO strike funds, the UFW was obliged to call off the lettuce strike wihout having regained its contracts from the Teamsters. A *New York Times Magazine* article in 1974 summed up the concerns of the union's supporters by its very title: "Is Chavez Beaten?" "No one who sympathizes with him," wrote the author, Winthrop Griffith, "wants to admit that he is defeated. Some of his Anglo supporters still pace the sidewalks in front of city supermarkets, imploring customers to boycott the grapes and lettuce inside, but their posture now indicates to the skeptical outsider that they are engaged in a lonely vigil, not a dynamic national movement."

It was perhaps inevitable that the farm workers' cause would lose some of its allure to the public, especially after five years had passed without a permanent solution to the farm labor struggles. But Chavez and the UFW were far from beaten. Indeed, a month before the *Times* article appeared, Richard Nixon, one of the UFW's archenemies, had resigned as president. Nixon had been implicated in the Watergate scandal, which stemmed from a 1972 burglary of the Democratic party's Washington headquarters. The new president, former vice-president Gerald Ford, was also a conservative Republican but had no particular ill will toward the farm workers.

More important, a significant change had taken place in California politics. Ronald Reagan had finished his second term, and the Democrats had won the 1974 election. The new governor was Edmund G. Brown, Jr., the 36-year-old son of former governor Pat Brown. Jerry Brown, as he was universally known, resolved to tackle the farm labor problem his father had always tried to sidestep. After extensive discussions with the unions and business groups, he put through the Agricultural Labor Relations Act, the first bill of rights for farm workers ever enacted in the United States.

The bill took effect in August 1975. By the fall, elections were being held all over California to determine whether the farm workers wished to be represented by the UFW, by the Teamsters, or by no union at all. With the new five-member Agricultural Labor Relations Board closely supervising the voting, the workers chose the UFW by a sizable margin, 53 percent to 30 percent for the Teamsters.

After many more months of negotiation, the Teamsters and the UFW finally came to terms. In March 1977, Chavez and Teamsters president Frank Fitzsimmons sat down in San Francisco to sign an agreement. Under the terms of the pact, the UFW would represent all workers whose employers were engaged in farming, even if those workers were truck drivers. The UFW expected that as a result its membership would increase from 25,000 to as many as 40,000. The

After more than a decade of bitter disputes, Teamsters president Frank Fitzsimmons (left) came to terms with the UFW. The agreement between the rival unions, signed on March 10, 1977, gave the UFW exclusive rights to organize field-workers.

Teamsters, for their part, would be free to organize workers in related industries, such as packing and processing. In an editorial applauding the settlement of the once-bitter dispute, the *New York Times* commented: "Cesar Chavez is jubilant, and Frank Fitzsimmons should also be pleased. The teamsters' eyes aren't quite as black as they used to be."

Now that the Teamsters had polished up their image, new opponents attempted to tarnish Chavez's reputation. In early 1979, farm workers' groups in Texas and Arizona charged that Chavez was trying to monopolize the farm workers' movement. They accused him of sabotaging their attempts to get federal funding so that they could set up independent unions. They also charged that his cousin Manuel had used union funds for his personal business dealings and that Chavez himself was intolerant of all opinions different from his own. Alfredo Avila, a former UFW organizer who had gone over to the Texas Farm Workers, complained: "The UFW is the only union I know of where there is no concept of a union local; everything comes from Cesar."

Workers' groups in Mexico added to the criticism by charging that during a 1974–75 strike in Yuma, Arizona, UFW people had severely beaten scores of Mexicans who had attempted to cross the border and work as strikebreakers.

Chavez responded by inviting a federal investigation into the UFW's finances. He stated his confidence that no irregularities would be found and maintained that his cousin Manuel (who had since left the union) had never engaged in any improper dealings.

Chavez conceded that UFW people had camped out along the Mexican border during the Yuma strike in 1974 and had turned back potential strikebreakers. But he vehemently denied that the union had employed violence to deter the Mexicans. Because investigators were unable to contact or interview the Mexicans who claimed to have been beaten, the issue was never resolved.

Though the critics were questioning some of Chavez's methods and complaining that he was unwilling to share power, none of them denied the effectiveness of his leadership. In the late 1960s, a farm worker had been lucky to earn as much as two dollars an hour. By 1980, the minimum wage specified in the UFW contracts was five dollars, plus benefits. By 1984, the 25,000 workers covered by the UFW were earning a minimum of $7 an hour, compared to the minimum of $5.30 paid to other farm workers.

Such rapid economic progress was bound to create a reaction. In 1983, the five-year agreement between the Teamsters and the UFW expired, and the Teamsters refused to renew the pact. Though they made no immediate move, the Teamsters reserved the right to resume their rivalry with the UFW in the future. In the political sphere, Jerry Brown had been replaced in the California statehouse by George Deukmejian, a conservative Republican.

Deukmejian's appointments to the Agricultural Labor Relations Board disappointed the UFW, which charged that the board had become overly sympathetic to the growers. By 1987, the union was so displeased with the board that it asked the California legislature to cut the board's funds. The legislature responded, slashing the appropriation by 25 percent.

At the same time, the union was increasingly concerned over the continued use of pesticides in the fields. The issue became especially urgent when a study conducted in McFarland, California, in the heart of the San Joaquin Valley, revealed higher-than-average rates of cancer for farm workers. In December 1987, Chavez appeared at a press conference with Ralph Nader, the longtime consumer advocate. With Nader's backing, Chavez called for a nationwide boycott of all grapes sprayed with five pesticides that had been judged potential health hazards by the U.S. Environmental Protection Agency—Dinoseb, captan, methyl bromide, parathion, and phosdrin. Using up-to-date techniques, the union organized the boycott by compiling computer lists of potential sympathizers and then mailing thousands of letters asking for support.

During the 1980s, the UFW became increasingly concerned about the use of dangerous pesticides in the grape orchards. Here, Chavez and Dolores Huerta express their views at a 1986 press conference in Fresno, California. The following year, the union began another boycott of California grapes.

Despite the gains made by Chavez and the UFW, many migrant farm workers still live in squalor. These California women, one of them pregnant, are forced to take shelter under a bridge along with 100 other homeless families.

Information was moving faster than it had at the union's birth, but the pace of social change had not kept up. Feeling that not enough progress was being made on the issues of vital concern to the farm workers, Chavez began his third major fast on July 17, 1988. This time, the national media paid only scant attention, but Spanish-language radio stations throughout the region broadcast daily bulletins on Chavez's condition. He was now 61 years old, and his doctors were more concerned than ever about his ability to withstand the rigors of the fast. At one point, the level of uric acid in Chavez's blood was three times what it should have been; despite the danger to his health, he persevered.

Twenty years had passed since the original fast that had helped make Chavez a national figure. Robert Kennedy's children did not forget. On the 36th and final day of the fast, Kerry Kennedy, Douglas Kennedy, and Kathleen Kennedy Townsend came to Delano with their mother to celebrate mass and express their

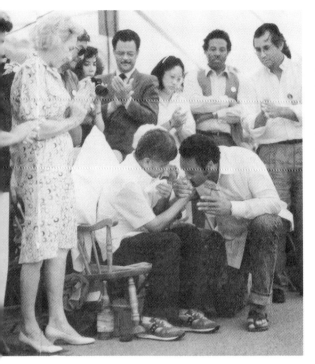

support for Chavez. Several thousand farm workers converged on Forty Acres and gathered under a huge tent erected to protect them from the blistering July sun. They saw Chavez, gray-haired and looking extremely weak, being helped to a chair on the platform by his sons Paul and Anthony. His 96-year-old mother, Juana, sat next to him. Along with the Kennedys, the rest of the Chavez family, and a group of celebrities including the actors Martin Sheen, Lou Diamond Phillips, and Edward James Olmos, Fred Ross stood behind Chavez on the platform. Ross had remained a constant friend and adviser since his first encounter with Chavez in Sal Si Puedes, 26 years before.

During the mass, Ethel Kennedy broke off a small piece of the semita and handed it to Chavez, just as her husband had done in 1968. The Reverend Jesse Jackson, a candidate for the 1988 Democratic presidential nomination, came forward to receive a small wooden cross from Chavez. Jackson accepted the cross as a token of his own pledge to fast for three days in support of the farm workers' cause. He declared: "I'll pick up the baton and carry it another lap; we'll keep passing that baton until justice comes to the workers!"

Chavez's own statement was read by his oldest son, Fernando, a member of the UFW's Attorneys Committee. "The fast will go on in hundreds of distant places," the statement concluded, "and it will multiply among thousands and then millions of caring people until every poisoned grape is off the supermarket shelves. And the fast will endure until the fields are safe for farm workers, the environment is preserved for future generations, and our food is once again a source of nourishment and life."

One hundred years before, Cesario Chavez, Cesar's grandfather, had brought his family across the Rio Grande to share a new life in the United States. Cesar Chavez had tried to enlarge that vision to include not only his own family but all his people. Chavez's dream had been so ambitious and his resources so modest that he was perhaps fated to appear, as he ended his fast in precarious health, as one who had fallen short of his goal. Undaunted, he regained his strength and continued to lead his union.

Alone among the electrifying figures who fired the social imagination of Americans during the 1960s—Martin Luther King, Jr., John and Robert Kennedy, Malcolm X—Cesar Chavez lived to grapple with the forces he had set in motion. In retrospect, he achieved as much in the field of civil rights as in the field of labor relations. Struggling not only for fair wages and decent working conditions, he also upheld the basic human dignity of Mexican Americans. His insistence on nonviolence, tolerance, and spiritual values did much to humanize a labor movement that was often criticized for caring too much about money and power.

In the midst of the Delano grape strike, Chavez told Peter Matthiessen: "*'Hay más tiempo que vida'* —that's one of our *dichos* [sayings]. 'There is more time than life.' We don't worry about time, because time and history are on our side." By dedicating his own life to changing the course of history, Cesar Chavez has made a unique contribution to American society.

Chronology

March 31, 1927	Born Cesar Estrada Chavez on a farm near Yuma, Arizona
1937–44	Chavez's parents lose everything in the depression; Chavez travels with his family, now migrant farm workers, throughout California
1944–46	Serves in the U.S. Navy during World War II
1948	Marries Helen Fabela
1952	Meets Fred Ross and goes to work for his Community Service Organization (CSO) on a voter registration drive
1959–62	Organizes farm workers throughout California's San Joaquin Valley into National Farm Worker's Association (NFWA); NFWA holds first convention in Fresno, California, fall 1962
1965	NFWA votes to strike against grape growers in California; Chavez speaks at Berkeley and other schools to drum up support for his cause; calls for a boycott against Schenley Industries, a major grape

	producer; AFL-CIO officially endorses the boycott at their convention
1966	Senator Robert F. Kennedy leads an investigation into the Delano strike, criticizes local officials for the treatment of the striking farm workers; Chavez and 66 other NFWA members embark on a 250-mile march to Sacramento from Delano to draw attention to the farm workers' plight; NFWA calls off boycott of Schenley after a settlement is reached, the first contract for farm workers in the United States; NFWA merges with AWOC to become United Farm Workers Organizing Committee (UFWOC)
March 1968	Chavez begins a fast to emphasize nonviolence in the continuing strike against the grape growers; ends the fast after 25 days and celebrates mass with Senator Kennedy
1969–70	Grape growers negotiate and settle with the union, and the strike officially ends on July 29, 1970; Chavez and UFWOC square off against the Teamsters, who try to organize lettuce workers in Salinas, California; Chavez sent to jail for refusing to lift boycott order against a major lettuce grower
1971	The Teamsters give up in Salinas after some of their members are indicted for misuse of funds and weapons possession
1972	Chavez fasts for 24 days in response to antiunion laws passed in Arizona; UFWOC is granted a charter by the AFL-CIO and changes name to United Farm Workers

August 1975   California governor Edmund G. "Jerry" Brown
                     signs the Agricultural Labor Relations Act, the first
                     bill of rights for farm workers ever enacted in the
                     United States

March 1977   Chavez and Teamsters president Frank Fitzsimmons
                     agree that the UFW will represent all farm workers

December 1987   Chavez and consumer advocate Ralph Nader urge
                     a boycott of all grapes sprayed with pesticides
                     deemed potentially hazardous by the U.S.
                     Environmental Protection Agency

1988   Chavez fasts for 36 days in support of the grape
                     boycott; pledges to continue the struggle until
                     workers achieve justice and grapes are safe to eat

Further Reading

Dunne, John Gregory. *Delano: The Story of the California Grape Strike.* Rev. ed. New York: Farrar, Straus & Giroux, 1971.

Dunning, Harold. *Trade Unions and Migrant Workers: A Worker's Educational Guide.* Washington: International Labor Office, 1985.

Fodell, Beverly. *Cesar Chavez and the United Farm Workers: A Selected Bibliography.* Detroit: Wayne State University Press, 1974.

Franchere, Ruth. *Cesar Chavez.* New York: Harper & Row, 1988.

Freeman, Richard. *What Do Unions Do?* New York: Basic Books, 1984.

Fusco, Paul, and George D. Horowitz. *La Causa: The California Grape Strike.* New York: Macmillan, 1970.

Galarza, Ernesto. *Farm Workers and Agri-Business in California, 1947–1960.* South Bend, IN: Notre Dame University Press, 1977.

Kushner, Sam. *Long Road to Delano.* Ann Arbor, MI: Books on Demand, N. d.

Levy, Jacques. *Cesar Chavez: Autobiography of La Causa.* New York: Norton, 1975.

Matthiessen, Peter. *Sal Si Puedes: Cesar Chavez and the New American Revolution.* Rev. ed. New York: Random House, 1973.

Roberts, Maurice. *Cesar Chavez and La Causa.* Chicago: Children's Press, 1986.

White, Florence. *Cesar Chavez: Man of Courage.* Champaign, IL: Garrard, 1973.

Index

CONSUELO RODRIGUEZ is a free-lance writer, lawyer, and union activist living in Texas. The daughter of migrant farm workers, she has written numerous articles on the labor movement in the United States and the Mexican-American experience.

RODOLFO CARDONA is professor of Spanish and comparative literature at Boston University. A renowned scholar, he has written many works of criticism, including *Ramón, a Study of Gómez de la Serna and His Works* and *Visión del esperpento: Teoría y práctica del esperpento en Valle-Inclán*. Born in San José, Costa Rica, he earned his B.A. and M.A. from Louisiana State University and received a Ph.D. from the University of Washington. He has taught at Case Western Reserve University, the University of Pittsburgh, the University of Texas at Austin, the University of New Mexico, and Harvard University.

JAMES COCKCROFT is currently a visiting professor of Latin American and Caribbean studies at the State University of New York at Albany. A three-time Fulbright scholar, he earned a Ph.D. from Stanford University and has taught at the University of Massachusetts, the University of Vermont, and the University of Connecticut. He is the author or coauthor of numerous books on Latin American subjects, including *Neighbors in Turmoil: Latin America, The Hispanic Experience in the United States: Contemporary Issues and Perspectives*, and *Outlaws in the Promised Land: Mexican Immigrant Workers and America's Future*.